PRIOR LEARNING
ASSESSMENT

PRINCIPLES

Marthe Sansregret, Ph.D.

HURTUBISE

HMH

Cover Design, Layout and Typesetting
Mégatexte inc.

Word Processing and English Translation
Hélène Laporte-Rawji Enr.

General Revision of the English Version
Karen Henchey

Canadian Cataloguing in Publication Data

Sansregret, Marthe

    Prior learning assessment: principles

    Translation of: La reconnaissance des acquis: principes.
    Includes bibliographical references.

    ISBN 2-89428-125-0

    1. Experiential learning - Evaluation. 2. College credits - Outside work - Evaluation. 3. Vocational qualifications - Certification. 4. Adult education. I. Title.

LC5219.S35213 1995   378.1'68   C95-941606-4

Éditions Hurtubise HMH ltée
7360 Newman Boulevard
LaSalle, Quebec
H8N 1X2
Canada
Telephone: (514) 364-0323
FAX: (514) 364-7435

ISBN 2-89428-125-0

Legal Deposit 4th trimester 1995
Bibliothèque nationale du Québec
National Library of Canada

© Copyright 1995 Éditions Hurtubise HMH ltée (Montreal)

© Copyright 1988 Éditions Hurtubise HMH ltée for the French version.

Printed in Canada

Distributed in Switzerland by GM DIFFUSION SA, Rue d'Etraz 2, CH-1027 Lonay, Switzerland / Tel.: (021) 803-26-26 / Fax: (021) 803-26-29.

This book is dedicated to those who would like to have their learning outcomes officially recognized as well as to those who commit their time and expertise to making this dream possible. It is important to mention in particular the major contribution the Council for Adult and Experiential Learning (CAEL) in the United States has made to the field of prior learning recognition and assessment.

I would also like to dedicate this book to my father and mother, individuals of principle with great hearts and minds.

ACKNOWLEDGEMENTS

I wish to express my gratitude to Professor Gabrielle Cantin from the Department of Andragogy of the University of Montreal. Professor Cantin helped me to structure the entire series and this specific book in particular. I will always feel indebted to her.

I would also like to thank Mrs. Hélène Laporte-Rawji for her assistance and help in preparing this document for publication.

PREFACE

The idea of giving formal recognition to the diversity of skills and knowledge that people acquire outside the formal settings of education and training has been gaining ground steadily for a generation. The 1980s were a particularly important decade in the development of the principles and practices that underpin the assessment of experiential and prior learning.

The English version of Marthe Sansregret's book, *La Reconnaissance des acquis: Principes,* is welcome because it lays out, in a practical and common-sense manner, the framework for tackling the assessment of prior learning that evolved during that period. It will be particularly helpful to administrators who are evaluating the implications of the recognition of prior learning for their institutions. It will also assist readers outside North America by giving them a perspective on the way thinking on this issue has developed in the USA and Canada.

The work rightly explores the ideological principles behind the recognition of prior learning before tackling the methodological issues. This exploration reminds us that to take account of prior learning is not just helpful to the student, it can also be an important developmental exercise for the institution and its staff. Assessing their prior learning helps us to understand, literally, where our students are coming from. It also challenges staff to be clear about how their institution itself adds value for students and to reflect on the nature of academic learning.

The advice that Dr. Sansregret distils from her research is eminently sensible. To be valuable to students the recognition of prior learning must be credible. This means that academic staff must be closely associated with the judgments that are made and they will require professional development for this task. For academics to prepare portfolios to present their own prior learning can be a useful exercise that helps them understand why the focus of portfolio assessment must be on learning outcomes—not on the portfolio itself.

The essential character of academic learning is that it is indirect. It is based on our experience of our experience of the world. This book shows how the preparation and assessment of a portfolio can make a significant contribution to the process of dialogue by which we come to understand what we have learned. In that sense the assessment of prior learning, if well done, can contribute to academic understanding just as much as anything that occurs in the classroom or the examination hall.

Sir John Daniel
Vice-Chancellor
The Open University
Milton Keynes, United Kingdom

FOREWORD

Universities, as institutions of higher education, have existed now for centuries and have taken on many roles and functions through the course of their history, but their ultimate mission resides essentially in providing an educated populace to society and to humanity as a whole. Universities are in the learning business, which most educators would agree can be achieved in different ways, whether through teaching, research activities, readings, or applied or work experiences. In fact, it is widely recognized that the styles and modes of learning vary enormously from one student to another and that what counts, ultimately, is not so much the how, when, what and where of learning, but the outcome, that is, what the individual has acquired in terms of knowledge, competencies and specific skills.

Educators responsible for the higher education of students try to build university programs that incorporate within the curriculum the appropriate mix of educational experiences (for example, courses, laboratories, research work, clinical practicum) that will set the stage for the student registered in that program to acquire both the depth and breadth of generic and specific knowledge/abilities deemed at a level of proficiency sufficient to the granting of a particular diploma or degree. Most would agree that it is not so much that a student must read a particular book, study a specific phenomenon or research a certain topic that is important, but that through these varied educational experiences, specific learnings do take place and that the cultivation of the mind is fully in progress and an ongoing process.

As the structure of today's labor market changes, requiring ever-increasing knowledge and skill levels among workers and professionals, institutions of higher education are facing a new challenge. They must adapt to the increasingly diverse educational paths of many of its citizens and keep pace with their desire and need for lifelong learning. Universities can no longer expect that their students will come from a single conventional entry channel and enrol into standard courses and programs tailored to the standard student, but that do not take into account the prior learnings of the lifelong learner. No contemporary society can afford to do "tabula rasa" with the prior learnings of any individual as he or she steps into a college or university—a situation that strongly beckons institutions to develop systematic methods of prior learning assessment that are both theoretically and scientifically sound.

It is in this respect that the writings of Dr. Marthe Sansregret will be most useful. In her book *Principles,* and the accompanying manual, *The Portfolio,* institutions and students are provided with a systematic and well-proven method to assess students' actual learnings and competencies on entry and on that basis give appropriate academic credits on which the student can then build to further his or her education. The reading of this book will be most valuable to all institutions committed to the idea of lifelong learning and to all learners in search of a theoretical and practical tool that will support them in their personal efforts to gain formal recognition for their prior learnings and thus facilitate their pursuit of continuous learning.

Dyane Adam, Ph.D.
Principal, Glendon College
York University
Toronto, Ontario

TABLE OF CONTENTS

Preface 7

Foreword 9

Introduction 15

**CHAPTER 1 — THE RESEARCH: FRAMEWORK
              AND METHODOLOGY** 17

THE RESEARCH PROJECT 19
    A Brief History 21
    The Research Problem 24
    Definitions 24
    Objective of the Research 25
    Value of the Research 26
    Type of Research 27

THE RESEARCH FRAMEWORK 27
    Conceptual Framework 27
    Operational Framework 29
        Research Questionnaire 29
        Preliminary Research 30
    Methodology 33
        Collecting the Data 33
        Analyzing the Data 34

CHAPTER 2 — IDEOLOGICAL PRINCIPLES 37

CHANGE 40
    Resistance to Change 44
    Adapting to Change 45

THE NEEDS OF ADULTS AND INSTITUTIONS 46

REASONS WHY ADULTS WANT TO HAVE THEIR
PRIOR LEARNING ASSESSED   48
  To Obtain an Academic Degree   49
  To Bring More Meaning to their Lives   52

REASONS FOR ACADEMIC INSTITUTIONS TO
ASSESS PRIOR LEARNING   53
  Guaranteeing the Reliability and Validity of the
  Accreditation   54
  Improving their Financial Situation   56
  Providing Teachers and Professors with
  a New Challenge   58

IDEOLOGICAL PRINCIPLES OF PRIOR LEARNING
ASSESSMENT   60

CHAPTER 3 — METHODOLOGICAL
                    PRINCIPLES   65

PLANNING THE PROGRAM   69
  Reasons and Motives   70
  Characteristics of the Program   71
  Developing and Organizing the Human Resources   .   76
  Admission Rules and Requirements   82
  Defining Students' Performance Criteria   84
  Rules for Granting Credits   85
  Financing the Program   86
  Advertising   89

IDENTIFICATION OF THE PRIOR LEARNING   90
  Characteristics of the Adult Student Clientele   90
  Methods to Identify the Learning   93
  The Portfolio Method   95

ASSESSMENT OF THE PRIOR LEARNING   104
  Choosing Assessors 105
  Suggested Criteria for Choosing Outside Experts   . . 107
  Assessments Based on the Judgments of Assessors   . 109

Choosing Assessment Procedures 111
Assessing the Learning Outcomes 112

ACCREDITATION 117
Accreditation in Practice 118
Transcripts 118
Accepting Credits Granted by Other Institutions . . . 123
Reviewing the Accreditation Process 123

METHODOLOGICAL PRINCIPLES OF PRIOR
LEARNING ASSESSMENT 124

Conclusion 129

Bibliography 133

Please Note: To avoid heaviness and repetition, the masculine gender has been used throughout this book.

INTRODUCTION

My goal in writing this book was to extract the principles governing the recognition of the various kinds of learning an adult acquires throughout his life, especially learning acquired outside traditional academic institutions. My objective was to identify the principles that are inherent in the literature, which originates in the United States for the most part. These principles have never been explicitly analyzed. Although the research that forms the basis of this book was conducted in the early eighties and my findings first published in 1988, the fundamental principles of prior learning assessment outlined in this book remain valid today.

The book is divided into three chapters. The first chapter explains how the research was conducted, outlining the framework and methodology used. The second chapter identifies the ideological principles of prior learning assessment. The chapter explains how the field of prior learning assessment came to be and the fundamental ideas behind it. The third chapter identifies the methodological principles—the ways institutions can put the ideological principles of prior learning into practice and develop prior learning assessment programs. By reading this book, then, you will learn how the field of prior learning assessment has developed, the fundamental principles that inform it, and some of the effective ways institutions can give an individual's prior learning the credit it merits.

CHAPTER

The Research: Framework and Methodology

CHAPTER 1

The Research: Framework and Methodology

THE RESEARCH PROJECT

Prior learning assessment, the process that enables adults and young adults alike to have some of the learning they acquired outside traditional schools officially recognized by academic institutions, is a phenomenon that is becoming increasingly important in the world of education today.

The phenomenon really began in the United States at the end of the Second World War. Since that time, it has been growing in popularity, particularly during the seventies. Researchers and educators have been working in the field of prior learning assessment for quite a number of years now; there are many articles, presentations, workshops, seminars, and conferences devoted to the subject. The public in general has begun to put more pressure on academic institutions regarding this most important question of recognizing prior learning.

Following the lead of the United States, Canada has shown a great deal of interest in prior learning recognition and assessment. Indeed, it has become important enough in Canada to be part of a series of recommendations made by a commission of inquiry, the *Commission d'étude sur la formation des adultes (la CÉFA)* (The Study Commission on Adult Education). In its final report, the Commission devoted an entire chapter to the recognition of prior learning, a field of adult education that is essential if institutions are to make themselves more accessible to the public. The Commission believes that a major transformation must occur in the education system in particular, and in society in general as well (Quebec 1982, p. 341).

Prior learning assessment has become particularly important in the province of Quebec. A colloquium entitled: "The Recognition of Experiential Learning in Universities . . . Why? How?" *(Reconnaître les acquis expérientiels à l'université . . . Pourquoi ?*

Comment ?) was held at the University of Sherbrooke in May 1985 for faculty, nonteaching professionals and administrators of French-speaking Canadian universities. At the colloquium, Mr. Pierre Moreault from the office of the Director General of University Teaching and Research *(Direction générale de l'enseignement et de la recherche universitaires)* made the following statement:

> More and more, universities are the privileged settings to practice prior learning assessment to answer the needs of a growing adult world that must submit to the risks of living in a society undergoing rapid change. . . . Universities do not have the choice: they must engage in accepting and efficiently evaluating the learning gained through experience. . . . What is involved is the credibility of the prior learning assessment system. This credibility is built on the mechanisms or effective and proven evaluation instruments and competent resource persons. It is the responsibility of competent universities to train resource persons for all levels of the education system and ensure the reliability of the evaluation tools (Moreault 1985).
>
> *[Translation]*

Among the various papers presented at the colloquium, one in particular insisted on the two pillars of prior learning assessment: the first being ideological and the second, methodological (Proulx).

At a conference of Canada's First Ministers held in Vancouver in November 1986, the Quebec deputy minister responsible for the status of women, Mrs. Monique Gagnon-Tremblay, recommended that it is a priority to recognize the learning women have acquired. This recognition would help women to return to school and paid employment (Gagnon-Tremblay).

On January 12, 1987, the Canadian government granted three million dollars to Quebec colleges for the purpose of studying the different aspects of the recognition of prior learning *(La Presse* and *The Gazette).*

Of course, interest in prior learning assessment is not limited to Canada and the United States. At the Fourth International Conference on Adult Education of the United Nations Educational,

Scientific, and Cultural Organization (UNESCO) held in March 1985, the following recommendation was made to the member states: to "take into account . . . the experience of the world acquired by the participants in their social, professional and cultural lives (UNESCO 1985, p. 65). . . . to promote the proper recognition of certificates awarded in non-formal education" (UNESCO 1985, p. 51). "Society should offer adults tailor-made programs covering the widest possible range of subjects and taking account of adults' existing knowledge and experience" (UNESCO 1985, p. 25). A journal on education entitled *Éducation permanente* published in Paris, France, has devoted an entire issue to the recognition of prior learning (No. 83-84/ June 1986. The title of the issue: *Reconnaître et valider les acquis* (Recognizing and Validating Acquired Learning)). In October 1986, the Glasgow College of Technology, located in Glasgow, Scotland, held its first workshop on prior learning assessment in order to facilitate and promote the access of adults to higher education (Sansregret).

In June 1987, a group of specialists in adult education from some 15 countries gathered at the First International Conference on Experiential Learning held in London, England. Following this conference, Switzerland, Venezuela and several others were added to the long list of countries that are seriously considering implementing a program of prior learning assessment. These countries see the implementation as a major short-term project for a society headed toward deep social change.

A BRIEF HISTORY

In the United States, the recognition of prior learning began about the year 1945. At that time, military personnel returning from the Second World War in large numbers became the first people to have their non-traditional learning recognized in order to facilitate their reintegration into civilian life.

While in military service, the military had to adapt to various circumstances, and acquired new knowledge in consequence.

This newly-acquired knowledge included know-how and new abilities. Many strongly believed that their acquired knowledge could help them find a new career and create a new life for themselves. The military were also aware of changes in their attitudes and behaviors and did not want to be given jobs merely on the basis of certificates or diplomas they acquired before the war.

Because they were conscious of the quality of their new learning and aware that it had equivalent value to that which was taught in traditional academic programs, the military put pressure on academic institutions and on various government departments. They sought recognition of their acquired knowledge and wanted assistance in finding suitable jobs in the labor market that matched their new skills. This was a historic occasion because it brought together the American government, academic institutions, community services, and the business world to tackle the problem. For the first time, the great partners of education and employment met to discuss the possibility of recognizing prior learning.

The result was that returning military personnel were offered a non-academic education given by teachers who normally taught in traditional schools. Courses were given off-campus, but what the military personnel were taught was often very similar to what was being taught in regular classrooms, often by the same teachers. In addition to this schooling, the military received a professional education. That is, they took courses that would enable them to acquire a new trade or career or gain access to one of the learned professions.

At the same time, academic institutions decided to conduct research to find ways to assess this new kind of learning that was revealed by the Second World War veterans. The American Council on Education (ACE) was urged by college presidents to "help develop a sound way in which colleges could recognize the learning of genuine college-course caliber that had been accomplished by service persons in World War II duty" (Spille 1980, p. 26). Because of the urgency of the request, some of the assessments were made while the research on prior learning assessment was being conducted.

As the service persons were making requests to have their specific situation studied carefully, the adult population in general was becoming more aware of the types of learning they had acquired through experience. The ensuing pressure from the general population forced academic institutions to seriously examine the question of assessment of non-formal, non-traditional learning. Needless to say, this new field of education attracted the interest of specialists in adult education, practitioners as well as researchers. A number of academic institutions conducted research and organized special projects and experiments, all with the specific objective of studying the question of prior learning assessment. The goals were to make recommendations, find solutions, develop practical methods, and working tools.

This sudden impetus to recognize prior learning put significant pressure on academic institutions: they had to rethink and readapt the academic system. What resulted was a proliferation of writings on many topics related to adult education. Some of these writings consider prior learning assessment from an educational point of view, attempting to clarify the notions of this field and present, define and analyze the inherent concepts and terminology. Other writings consider prior learning assessment from the point of view of disciplines, specialities, and places of work.

The high-quality work of individuals and teams from various fields of adult education contributed to the advancement of this new branch in education. The literature was very heterogeneous, and as the years went by, a common vocabulary came to be adopted and used. Also, a number of rules related to the ideology and sometimes the methodology emerged. These rules evolved and became standards over time.

At present, it is often difficult to pinpoint all of these rules. Sometimes they take the form of statements, presentations, recommendations or propositions that have never been identified explicitly, but that seem to have gained consensus throughout the entire field of prior learning assessment.

THE RESEARCH PROBLEM

A number of conclusions emerge from the experience of reading the now extensive literature on prior learning assessment. The most significant conclusion to be drawn, perhaps, is that the literature seems to lack an unequivocal explanation of the practice of prior learning assessment. This study attempts to do just that. This study of the principles of prior learning assessment approaches the literature by asking the following question: What are the principles governing the recognition of prior learning? The objective of this study, then, is to identify the principles governing prior learning assessment according to the motives and reasons revealed in the American literature on the subject in the hope that these findings will help those involved in prior learning assessment programs today.

DEFINITIONS

To begin, the words "prior learning," "the recognition of prior learning" and "principles" need to be explained in detail.

PRIOR LEARNING

According to Rydell, prior learning is an accumulation of skills recent enough that their depth and breadth can be easily demonstrated and verified by an expert. Seeman defines prior learning as the skills a person has acquired to reproduce an experience with cognitive and affective perceptions. Cross goes as far as saying that experiential learning or prior learning is "the term that has come into being to reflect widespread agreement that when or where or from whom one learns is not nearly as important as what one learns" (Cross 1978, p. 8).

This study defines prior learning as the learning that comes mainly from experience; it is, as Breen, Dunlon and Whitaker define it, the learning "which occurs without the awareness or sanction of the institution, and in a non-academic setting" (Breen and others 1977*a,* p. 9).

THE RECOGNITION OF PRIOR LEARNING

The recognition of prior learning is the identification, assessment and accreditation of experiential learning (Spille). To Knapp and Forrest, the recognition of prior learning means identifying, assessing and giving credit to learning that comes from experience. Knapp and Jacobs define the recognition of prior learning as a process by which experiential learning is identified, assessed and credited in relation to courses of a specific academic level. According to Willingham, the recognition of prior learning is a process by which we try to identify the portion of learning that someone has acquired in relation to existing courses and programs that lead to a degree.

The 1982 report of the Study Commission on Adult Education states that the assessment of prior learning comes from outside the academic milieu and judges or recognizes a capacity, a skill that a person or a group of individuals has acquired. According to the report, then, prior learning assessment has, therefore, a social as well as a legal dimension (Quebec 1982, p. 342).

PRINCIPLES

Dictionaries give three different definitions of the word "principle" (Bordas, Larousse, Quillet, Oxford, and Webster). Sometimes the word can mean fundamental, origin, source or starting point. It can also signify a rule or law and finally, a motive or reason. It is mainly this latter meaning, that is, a motive or reason, that defines the way "principle" is used in this book.

OBJECTIVE OF THE RESEARCH

As was stated above, the objective of this study is to identify the principles governing prior learning assessment according to the motives and reasons discovered in the American literature, most significantly the literature published from the early seventies to the mid eighties.

VALUE OF THE RESEARCH

This study will have the advantage of regrouping into one volume all the information now dispersed throughout the literature on prior learning assessment. This could prove valuable to a good number of people.

Administrators, counselors and assessors working in academic institutions certainly wish to grasp the ideology and understand the methodology of prior learning assessment before embarking in this new process.

In addition to academic institutions, professional organizations and other comparable providers of education wish to comprehend the reasons why adults want to have their prior learning assessed as well as the reasons why institutions would be interested in assessing it. If such non-academic institutions could have an idea of the process in which academic institutions are getting involved when assessing prior learning, they could devise parallel plans to work in cooperation with these academic institutions in such activities as credited professional development. Professional associations who at this moment are considering redefining or revising their admission criteria could then use the results of this research to determine their membership criteria.

This research could also motivate union leaders to recognize the prior learning of their members. Institutions who usually give non-traditional education would also find in it a new source of information.

And finally, the results of this research would provide a general overview of what changes and adaptations academic institutions and adults will have to make to recognize prior learning.

TYPE OF RESEARCH

In general, the literature explains and justifies the necessity for academic institutions to assess prior learning. Some writers focus more on the motives or reasons why institutions could make the decision to implement a program of prior learning assessment, while others describe the process and various methods used in the field.

All of these reasons or motives, as well as the methods to assess prior learning are discussed in the literature, but nowhere are the principles identified as such. Therefore, this research of the American literature published primarily from 1970 to 1986 is an exploratory type of research.

THE RESEARCH FRAMEWORK

The latter part of Chapter 1 introduces the conceptual and operational frameworks guiding this research and explains how the data was collected and studied.

CONCEPTUAL FRAMEWORK

Regardless of what some may wish to say to the contrary, it has always been possible to learn at any age (Cross), place and time, and in any way, by any means and in any field (Keeton and Tate). Society has always attributed a value to experiential learning acquired outside of school on an ongoing basis or at different times in life. Learning through experience created the possibility for adults to live according to a model designed for them either by religion, their family or society in general (Keeton and Tate). The value ascribed to this type of learning has always been part of philosophers' thinking, from ancient times to the present day. As Fox wrote in 1981, the concept to recognize experiential learning is certainly not new, but dates as far back as the *Dialogues of Socrates,* the medieval guides and is evident more recently in the modern theories of Whitehead and Dewey, for example.

Although society has never denied the importance of learning by experience, our modern society is more inclined to assign higher value to a different type of learning, learning acquired through a theoretical approach (Keeton and Tate). Schools have been given the mandate to teach and assess the learning acquired by young students in a definite setting, according to a specific schedule and predetermined methods and content. As a result, this new way of defining learning has created two different worlds: one for the young who learn through theory, and the other for adults who learn experientially more often than not.

The baby boom has been over for a few decades now; there are fewer and fewer young students in schools. At the same time, adults who left school years ago are now deciding to return. Indeed, they are returning to school in larger numbers than ever, and they register in a wide range of courses.

For all kinds of reasons, adults feel that they need to learn through theory in order to complement their practical experience. They believe that they have the right to have their experiential learning recognized and assessed. They would like academic institutions to give them the opportunity to learn by building on the basis of what they know already, and not be obliged to take courses on subjects they already master.

Fulfilling this wish on the part of returning adults to have their prior learning credited by academic institutions is not part of the traditional mandate schools received from society, which is to teach and assess learning acquired in a formal setting. Therefore, this request questions once more the traditional way by which academic institutions think and operate.

Academic institutions are now facing a new situation where they have to question the reasons why they would change the nature of their mandate and the ways and means they have at their disposal to answer the new expectations of adults. Before responding to the requests from the adult population, academic institutions want to clarify their own reasons or motives as well as those of the adults. Once institutions can justify the implementation of a prior learning assessment program, other issues will be raised regarding the planning, the decision-making process, and the organization and procedure to implement the program.

These questions facing academic institutions are essentially of an ideological and methodological nature. An analysis of these questions leads to the discovery of the governing principles inherent in the literature. These principles underlie the practice of prior learning today, and they should establish that methodology is influenced by ideology to a certain degree.

OPERATIONAL FRAMEWORK

This section describes how the research was conducted. It outlines the research method used to approach the prior learning assessment literature, including the questions the study sought to answer.

RESEARCH QUESTIONNAIRE

Before the study of the prior learning assessment literature could begin, a research method had to be developed. The research instrument chosen was a questionnaire consisting of two main questions. The first question was of an ideological nature; the second, of a methodological nature. These two main questions generated other questions, which ultimately resulted in the research instrument.

Questions on Ideology

The main ideological question is: What are the ideological principles of prior learning assessment? The answer to this question is somewhere in the literature and to find it, the research instrument included a couple of subquestions that take into consideration the fact that prior learning assessment is a great concern to both adults and academic institutions. The subquestions therefore read as follows:

— What are the reasons or motives claimed in the literature in the name of adults to assess prior learning?

— What are the reasons or motives claimed in the literature in the name of institutions to assess prior learning?

Questions on Methodology

The main methodological question formulated is: What are the methodological principles governing the practice of prior learning assessment? Because these principles are not specifically identified in the literature and because the methods differ in practice, a series of subquestions are used to help answer the question. They are:

— What are the existing methods used to assess prior learning?

— Does each method deal with the entire process of the recognition of prior learning, with respect to the definition given above?

— Is there one method that is more useful than another? If so, what are the different stages and operations of this method?

— Can a link between the ideological and the methodological principles be identified in this study of the various stages in the process of prior learning assessment?

PRELIMINARY RESEARCH

Once a questionnaire with which to approach the literature was developed, the preliminary research could begin. The preliminary research made to compile the prior learning assessment literature is described below.

Stage 1 – Searching the Documents

The search for relevant documents on prior learning assessment began with a data collection using the Educational Resources Information Center (ERIC) Data Bank on Adult, Career and

Vocational Education of the United States Department of Education. The data was collected using 10 key words or expressions. They are, in alphabetical order:

adult
experiential learning
job
learning by doing
methodology
models
portfolio
principles
recognition
vocational education

The search found 598 documents, which covered the period from the early seventies to the mid eighties, and especially the period from 1974 to 1986. Most of the documents found described the results of research or experiments that had been conducted.

A quick glance of the abstracts in the first data collection revealed two important sources of information in the field of prior learning. The first is a 22-volume set published by the Cooperative for the Assessment of Experiential Learning (CAEL) of Columbia (Maryland), which later became the Council for the Advancement of Experiential Learning (CAEL) and most recently, the Council for Adult and Experiential Learning (CAEL). The 22 CAEL publications were published in the eight years from 1975 to 1982. CAEL also published the following books: *Bridging the Gap* by Breen and Whitaker, published in 1983, and Simosko's *Earn College Credit for What You Know,* published in 1985.

CAEL published a good deal of material until 1982. Since that time, the number of yearly publications put out by the Council has diminished somewhat. Indeed, the following observation was made at the annual general assembly of the Council held in November and December of 1986: "The current theory base [for CAEL's work] needs updating. CAEL's contributions around basic theory came ten or so years ago, and . . . there hasn't been much since to which you can direct newcomers" (p. 6). The original CAEL research is still being used by many academic institutions, a fact that is revealed by the numerous references to and comments made on CAEL material in other documents found in the preliminary data search.

CAEL is a research and documentation center that came into being through a project undertaken by the Educational Testing Service (ETS) of Princeton, New Jersey. Today the Center consists of more than 500 institutional and individual members who, because of the Center, now have the possibility to exchange information with their fellow colleagues. Since its foundation in 1974, CAEL rapidly developed into an information network to support researchers and ultimately help to coordinate, publish and disseminate the work of its members.

The second important source of information found in the data search is a series of 24 volumes published by Jossey-Bass Incorporated under the title, *New Directions for Experiential Learning*. They are edited by individuals who are all members of CAEL. A quarterly publication from 1978 to 1983, the *New Directions for Experiential Learning* series examines prior learning assessment from different angles and themes. Each volume analyzes a specific aspect of prior learning assessment from various viewpoints, and a principal editor comments on the information discussed. The main objective of this series is to summarize the most recent knowledge and practices to advance the understanding of experiential learning within the education system (Keeton and Tate).

Stage 2 – Making an Inventory and Selecting the
            Documents

In the prior learning assessment literature, the expression "experiential learning" has two broad meanings: the first is supervised learning (acquired through apprenticeships or internships), which corresponds to a learning-by-doing approach; the second is non-supervised learning, which is acquired mainly outside a classroom, that occurs without the supervision of a professor or teacher. The second definition of experiential learning, which most people call "prior learning," is the type of experiential learning relevant for this study. Therefore, all the abstracts dealing with supervised learning were eliminated from the list.

Another problem encountered in the research was the different meanings given to the words "evaluation" or "assessment." Sometimes the words are used to describe the entire process of recognizing prior learning; other times, they are used to identify the operation to assess the learning outcomes, that is, only one stage of the entire process.

The works listed in the bibliography at the end of the book come from these three sources: the ERIC Data Bank, CAEL and *New Directions for Experiential Learning.* Along with these works dealing with prior learning assessment, the bibliography lists other works that were valuable for this study.

METHODOLOGY

The following pages contain a brief description of how the documents used in this study were dealt with once the initial search and selection was made.

COLLECTING THE DATA

Having made an initial selection of the documents, the next step was to read each document systematically. It soon became obvious that the three sources, ERIC, CAEL and *New Directions for Experiential Learning,* are very different in content and presentation. For example, in the *New Directions for Experiential Learning* series, authors summarize different aspects of prior learning assessment. Articles are written, edited and presented on specific topics, which vary from one volume to the next.

With the CAEL publications, the presentation varies according to the objectives, topics and authors. In some cases, a document is signed by one author; in others, by a team of authors. Sometimes the publication is a reference or working document; at other times, it is a handbook.

The literature in the ERIC Data Bank includes a large number of presentations from various conferences, seminars and the like. The data bank also contains a tremendous amount of research reports and reports on experiments conducted as well as handbooks and guides.

All the documents were initially read to obtain a general overview of their contents. Then a second, more selective reading was made, using the research questionnaire developed. Each statement that seemed to help answer a question was noted on index cards.

ANALYZING THE DATA

All the information collected on the index cards was then systematically studied in the five operations described below.

First Operation: Content Analysis

In the first operation, all statements collected were read and interpreted within their respective contexts and catalogued according to the two main categories in the questionnaire, that is, ideology and methodology. Second, the statements within these two main categories were further grouped according to similarity and complementarity factors.

Second Operation: Looking for the Reasons

Once the statements that seemed to answer the research questions were gathered, the next step was to search the literature for the justification of the statements, which elucidated the underlying ideology and orientation governing the practice as well as the research.

Third Operation: *Preliminary Classification*

This third operation consisted of grouping related statements into general themes and classifying these themes into one of the two main categories. Because they were easier to identify given their practical nature, the themes related to the methodological category were collected first. Then the themes related to the ideological category were grouped together. These themes covered the explanations, justifications and reasons behind prior learning assessment.

Fourth Operation: *Organizing the Content and Results*
                         According to the Ideological
                         Principles

Once all the themes dealing with ideology were put together, their interrelationship was studied. Possible links emerged among the themes. Next, the information was organized into a logical set of reasons for prior learning assessment claimed by adults and academic institutions. From a thorough examination of the context surrounding the reasons or motives and therefore the needs and expectations of prior learning assessment, the ideological principles were identified.

Fifth Operation: *Organizing the Content and Results*
                        According to the Methodological
                        Principles

The statements found in the literature that relate to the methodological principles of prior learning were classified according to the subquestions of the questionnaire. The answers to the subquestions helped to sort out the chronological steps of the prior learning assessment process: identification, assessment and accreditation. In the end, it was possible to identify the methodological principles by analyzing the advice, warnings and recommendations contained in the literature. The underlying message in the advice, warnings and recommendations established a strong link between method and ideology, a link that is evident in this study.

In sum, this introductory chapter shows how the research project got underway: it explains how the prior learning assessment literature was initially selected and the systematic questionnaire used to isolate the ideological and methodological principles inherent in the literature. The next two chapters explore the findings of this study, beginning with the ideological question.

CHAPTER

Ideological Principles

CHAPTER 2

Ideological Principles

This chapter is devoted entirely to the identification of the ideological principles of prior learning assessment revealed in the extensive literature on the subject. The chapter answers the main ideology question raised in Chapter 1: What are the ideological principles of prior learning assessment?

Historically, requests for the assessment of non-traditional learning such as those made by American soldiers and later by the American population in general paved the way for an alliance between the state, academic institutions, volunteer organizations and the business world to study the possibilities of prior learning assessment. This alliance was very important because it questioned the mandate that society had given to academic institutions, the mandate which made the institutions responsible for teaching and assessing whatever was learned theoretically by children and teenagers. According to this mandate, academic institutions would ultimately issue a diploma to confirm the quality of the young person's learning, a diploma that also gave its holder easier access to the job market and automatically granted him status within society.

Times have changed. Families are now smaller and fewer students are registered in academic institutions in consequence. The young student population is being replaced by adults (Gray and Davis). Men and women who never had the option of completing a degree program in a traditional school are more and more enthusiastic and motivated with the idea that their prior learning could be recognized and assessed. This would enable them to return to school and study, building on the groundwork of what they know already (Scott).

According to a study conducted by Cross, the number of adults who request admission in classes and enroll in such activities as workshops and group discussions is far greater than the total number of regular students registered in post-secondary schools. Adults studying on a part-time basis are now the new majority on campus (Cross).

The end of the baby boom and the return of adults to school are two phenomena that reflect change, a characteristic of our time. Indeed, change and its consequences is a common theme running through the prior learning assessment literature. People's needs change and so do those of academic institutions, and these facts help to justify the need for prior learning assessment. Adults and academic institutions have their respective reasons and motives for wanting to see prior learning assessment become a reality in a world where few things remain stable.

This chapter identifies and presents the ideological principles of prior learning assessment as they are revealed in the literature. The most frequently discussed themes are analyzed in order to understand their full importance as well as their interrelationship. These themes are: change, resistance to change, the possibility of adapting to change, the needs of adults and institutions to grow in a constantly changing society, and the reasons adults and academic institutions have for requesting and granting the recognition of prior learning. A thorough study of these themes leads to the identification of the ideological principles of prior learning assessment.

CHANGE

Change is a phenomenon that disturbs the habits of individuals and groups, disrupting their ways of doing or being. According to Boucouvalas, change is a characteristic of our time and it is shaking the very foundations of society. The consequences are perhaps as significant as those that provoked the passage from an agrarian to an industrialized society.

Change has become so important in the everyday life of adults and institutions that it has modified not only our way of living, but it has in itself become a way of living, thus spawning the notion of change as a way of life (Axford).

As Kanfer and Goldstein state, we are continuously bombarded by ideas, choices and objectives from the media and the world around us, and at the end of any given day, every individual has undergone a change for better or for worse. As Kanfer and Goldstein write: "A conversation with a friend, an interesting movie or a book, a new emotional experience, a political rally, a work of art, or a breathtaking natural scene may all make a deep impression on us and can alter our attitudes about ourselves and about the world" (Kanfer and Goldstein 1975, p. 1). Our homes have been invaded by telecommunications. Personal computers and videocassettes are now becoming as essential to the home as the television and the telephone were in the past (Matusak).

Of course, the rate at which change occurs varies depending on the field of activity. In 1977, Knox commented that change occurs more rapidly in the fields of science and technology, but is more moderate in the aspects of life that affect personal values, employment or housing, for instance. Change is typically more rapid and more intense in fields related to economics than in those related to politics or social evolution. Knox also points out that all change is not necessarily an indication of progress; think of all the problems generated by pollution, which itself is a product of advances in technology.

In academic institutions, change has affected the traditional way things have always been done. Post-secondary institutions are apparently in a state of confusion and seem at present undecided as to which direction they will take (Bradley and Bolman). The world of education, just as the working society, has been unprecedentedly transformed over the past 35 years (Kyle). A survey conducted on the population of the state of Maine revealed that the number of adults wishing to return to school is exceeding by far the total number of registrations in all the state colleges and universities (Moon and Hawes).

While younger students usually study full-time, three quarters of the adults who wish to return to school across the United States opt for part-time studies (Cross). Part-time studies are

popular (Warren) because they allow adults to continue working, which in turn enables them to fulfill their fundamental
needs of acquiring food, clothing and a place in which to live
(Jacobs and Allen).

Some of the literature reports that women are at the center of
this phenomenon of change because they are returning to
school in such large numbers. Indeed, some writers estimate
that women constitute two thirds of the new adult student population (Fisher-Thompson; Ekstrom) and that the majority of
these women are 30 years of age and older (Scott). Other
authors do not provide specific statistical data, but state nevertheless that women constitute an important part of the new
student clientele (Eliason; Neely and Steffen; Ekstrom;
Menson; Smythe and Jerabek). Their numbers are constantly
growing (Mahoney) and so too are the number of adults who
hope to make a career change (Mark and Menson).

The phenomenon of change brings about one third of the active
American population to participate each year in formal education (Cross) in addition to those adults who register in
independent studies (Dwyer and Torgoff; Stanley). These
returning adults have learned quite a few things by themselves,
and 80% of them undertake at least one learning project per
year (Tough; Penland). Some adults devote approximately
100 hours of study every year for each learning project, and
they sometimes undertake as many as five learning projects per
year (Cross).

The massive influx of adults has forced academic institutions to
consider the prospect of radically changing their traditional
mandate. Because schools must now open their doors to adults
who claim to have learned many things in a non-traditional
way, that is, through experience, schools can no longer expect
to teach and evaluate all their students the same way and expect
all their new students to be at exactly the same academic level.
Indeed, the adults showing up at the doors of academic institutions are of all ages, origins, races, backgrounds and have
different experiences (Knapp; Christopulos and Hafner) and

different needs (Reinharz; Mahoney; Wingard; Chickering). The experiential learning these returning adults have acquired is so important that several writers mention the works of Coleman and others who said that in order to be fair to adults, two learning styles should be considered: one practical and the other theoretical (Taylor; Smith). Other writers support the idea and discuss the research made by Kolb, who maintains that the traditional way of learning promotes the development of skills and the perception of symbols, while experiential learning fosters the acquisition of affective and behavioral skills (Doherty and others).

Depending on the experiential learning involved, an adult may acquire up to four main skills: he lives a concrete experience, observes it, draws abstractions, concepts and generalizations, and then proceeds with the experimentation (Fry and Kolb). Kolb and Lewis write: "An affective environment emphasizes the experiencing of concrete events; a symbolic environment emphasizes abstract conceptualization; a perceptual environment stresses observation; and a behavioral environment stresses action taking" (Kolb and Lewis 1986, p. 100). The recognition of experiential learning then proves to be a more equitable process for adults because it enables them to learn according to the style that suits them best and to complete the theoretical learning that is lacking in their education (Laudeman).

Some of the learning experiences adults have lead them to reach a high level of knowledge on the scale of cognitive skills developed by Bloom in 1956 (Mahoney). Other types of learning experiences belong in the affective domain, as it was defined by Bloom in 1956 and again in 1971 and by Krathwohl and others in 1956 (Greenblatt and Striby; Chickering). By recognizing experiential or prior learning, schools would be fair to adults, enabling them to complete the theoretical knowledge that is missing in their education, since traditional schools focus more on theory than on practice (Whitaker).

RESISTANCE TO CHANGE

No adult reacts the same way when confronted with change. Some feel very insecure and would like things to remain always as they were because they feel lost in a world where things are constantly evolving (Bergevin).

Senior citizens, for example, are often unwilling to accept change because they feel that time is going by too quickly and that at their age they can no longer learn anything new. On this subject of change and the willingness to accept change, Bergevin writes: "While such resistance appears in us at all ages, it usually becomes more pronounced as we grow older. Older persons generally experience less affectivity and are faced with the reality that they dispose of less time to get what they need and want; consequently, they think they must hold on to what they have" (Bergevin 1967, p. 93).

There are also those who are unable to change their way of thinking and doing (Knox). Others resist change by adopting a rigid attitude, or by feeling threatened or acting aggressively. These people usually find little happiness or satisfaction in life and are not yet able to find ways to adjust in order to improve their own situation (Knox).

Again, both academic institutions and adults have to face change. The prior learning assessment requested by adults tends to upset the habits of academic institutions. Sweet insists that academic institutions do not have a choice any more, and that to ignore these changes and their alternative solutions at this time would present a great danger for their future. Sweet foresaw that academic institutions who refused to adapt would have to face a possible reduction of their student clientele because they would redirect their requests to such other providers of learning as non-traditional schools, the state, employers, community associations, and unions.

ADAPTING TO CHANGE

While some adults and institutions undoubtedly resist change, there are nevertheless those who are willing to try to adapt. Indeed, some adults see change as an opportunity to allow themselves the luxury to think in order to better understand what is happening and then take the appropriate measures to orient their choices to the new situation (Bergevin).

In 1970, Knowles wrote that a society in which change affects its economic and technological sectors in addition to its political, social, cultural and theological environment needs citizens who are able to change. Knowles goes further by stating that a society whose geographic, economic, and intellectual aspects are becoming increasingly complex and interdependent requires citizens capable of expanding their way of seeing the world, acquiring wider and broader knowledge. Indeed, the citizens are required to be more tolerant and have greater interpersonal skills than the citizens of previous societies were ever required to possess (Knowles 1970, p. 32). Knowles adds that a society in which machinery does more and more of the work traditionally performed by people requires citizens capable of performing increasingly complex tasks and capable of filling their newly-acquired leisure time. Knowles continues by writing that in a society where the differences between people (youths and adults, blacks and whites, East and West, rich and poor) are becoming more defined and less tolerated requires citizens who are capable of ridding themselves of the traditional prejudices and able to establish open, empathetic and collaborative relationships with everyone, regardless of race, background or color (Knowles 1970, p. 32-33).

For traditional institutions, adapting to change means facing and winning a new challenge since they have the responsibility to prepare people to live and work in a society that has to face unforeseeable, constant and disturbing transformations (Greenberg).

In the prior learning assessment literature, a great deal of emphasis is placed on the human being and his need to adapt. In adapting to change, adults learn many new things that they wish to have recognized by academic institutions. Institutions are more and more willing to answer these requests and are seeking new ways of doing so (Luskin and Small) by developing new programs and offering new services that would cater to the needs of adults (Holt; Thomas and others).

THE NEEDS OF ADULTS AND INSTITUTIONS

Much of the prior learning assessment literature reveals, sometimes implicitly, sometimes explicitly, the writers' desire to understand the needs of adults and appreciate how important these needs are. This concern with the needs of adults is evident, for example, in the works of Van Aalst, Shipton and Steltenpohl, as well as Reichlin, who all base their discussions on Maslow's theories. Indeed, Maslow's writings have a significant influence on how those who write about prior learning assessment define needs and therefore deserve a closer look. The following synthesis of Maslow's considerable work is based on Tétrault's and Alpalhaô's analyses of Maslow's writings.

Even in his early writings, Maslow shows a strong will to make his readers aware of people's needs. Later, in 1962, he became more specific on the topic of needs, saying that they could be divided into two large categories: fundamental and developmental needs (Tétrault). Maslow observes that it is essential for an adult to fulfill his fundamental needs; otherwise, he would be unable to gain access to a higher level of development. Such fundamental/basic maintenance needs as feeding, keeping warm, sleeping and attaining sexual satisfaction belong to the physiological level. When these needs are fulfilled, an individual can sustain himself throughout his life. While the degree to which each of these basic needs must be satisfied varies from person to person, the needs are the same for all human beings. If for some reason these basic needs are not satisfied, then the individual lacks the proper motivation to move ahead and satisfy other additional needs.

When his fundamental needs have been satisfied, the individual tries to satisfy his other needs, his developmental needs. The developmental needs can vary from one person to the next. Here are some examples of what a person's developmental needs might be: the need for security, belonging, love and esteem. How important each developmental need is depends on the individual and his sense of responsibility, his ambitions and what he wants to accomplish in his life (Alpalhaô).

Unlike the fundamental needs, which are relatively similar for everyone and have a limited reach, a person's developmental needs are highly individual and can satisfy not only a person's way of doing, but his way of being (Alpalhaô). Once an individual has fulfilled his fundamental needs, he might wish to achieve a social ideal, while another may seek higher monetary rewards in life. A person's needs can touch all aspects of his life, depending on how he interprets his needs and how he tries to satisfy them.

In the revised edition of *Motivation and Personality,* published in 1970, Maslow writes: "Human life will never be understood unless its highest aspirations are taken into account. Growth, self-actualization, the striving toward health, the quest for identity and autonomy, the yearning for excellence (and other ways of phrasing the striving 'upward') must by now be accepted beyond question as a widespread and perhaps universal human tendency" (Maslow 1970, p. xii-xiii).

It is possible to apply Maslow's hierarchy of needs to institutions as well. For example, institutions need a stable clientele, a permanent staff, a suitable location and good buildings. These, then, would be the institution's maintenance or fundamental needs. Institutions also try to offer an increasingly higher quality service (Keeton). This could be interpreted as the institution's developmental needs. Both sets of needs can be difficult to satisfy when the economy of the society in which the institution exists is not good (Johnson and Tornatzky).

The prior learning assessment literature shows that adults and academic institutions have specific reasons to see prior learning assessment as a way to satisfy their needs.

REASONS WHY ADULTS WANT TO HAVE THEIR PRIOR LEARNING ASSESSED

Adults will experience change each in their own way, according to their very specific needs. It has been observed that adults can learn better when what they are learning is somehow familiar to them and they are usually more motivated to learn when they are active participants in the learning process. They are more inclined to integrate and use material that reflects their own language and their own experience (Smith).

When adults make a first attempt to return to school, they are often disappointed to see that it is often not equipped to answer their needs, the school catering instead to the needs of younger students (Stanley; Smythe and Jerabek; Foster and others; Holt). However, adults believe that they have acquired a large amount of information and would like to be treated with justice and fairness (Martorana and Kuhns).

Adults wonder what the use is of having all their acquired learning when they are forced to relearn over and over again what they know already. Therefore, they would like academic institutions to take into consideration what they have learned throughout their lives so that they may study only what they do not know, which would allow them to move ahead faster and learn more. Adults want institutions to look at their individual situation and assess the results of what they have learned so far. They wish to see institutions develop the proper tools to help them evaluate the kind of learning they have acquired (Green and Sullivan; Davis and Knapp; Reinharz; Mahoney; Chickering). They also expect institutions to provide them with the necessary help that would enable them to demonstrate the evidence of what they know.

Among the reasons given in the literature to recognize and assess prior learning, the most common ones are the desire of adults to obtain an academic degree and give meaning to their lives.

TO OBTAIN AN ACADEMIC DEGREE
(attestation, certification, diploma, qualifications, etc.)

Most often, the primary reason adults give for having their learning properly assessed is to obtain a degree. They believe that having the academic degree will improve their chances of finding a better job, do justice to the training they have undergone, and allow them to reach a higher social status.

The world is undergoing rapid and often unpredictable change. Today more than ever, a person is less sure to keep his first job permanently. Back in 1969, Toffler predicted that those who enter the labor market in the seventies would probably have to change jobs or even fields of competence more than once over a period of 20 to 30 years. Adults are now forced to acquire new learning in order to adjust to the changes around them and prepare themselves for new kinds of tasks, even to the point of making a career change.

Often when adults go job hunting, they have to prove their prior learning. If they do not hold a degree, it could mean their chances of success are decreased because most employers still base their employment selection on the degrees the applicant holds (Martorana and Kuhns). Adults feel strongly that having a degree puts them in a strong position *vis-à-vis* the potential employer (De Meester; Marienau and Chickering). A degree is not only the official recognition that a person has acquired certain academic skills, but a passport in a constantly changing society that is becoming more and more specialized, a society in which judging the competence of a person is becoming increasingly difficult (Christensen; Harris and Troutt). Moreover, the academic prerequisites to qualify for a job are increasing. Hogan writes: "Today it is not uncommon for many occupations to require a master's degree and several require a doctorate" (Hogan 1979, p. 16). Sometimes too, people are required to possess a specific academic diploma before they are allowed to practice in a specific career or profession (Hatala). In essence, the world of business and industry requires a higher than ever level of education and adults who hold a degree happen to hold a proof of learning that is acknowledged by employers (Kyle).

Finding and keeping a job have become increasingly important preoccupations for adults. This makes possessing an academic degree all the more important because of its link to success in the world of work. Adults who have never worked before now have to find a job in order to cope with heavier financial obligations. Knapp predicts that "the external economy and inflation will force people who have never worked before to work and those who work will have to change their jobs and careers a number of times or become recertified, indicating the need for more education and training to qualify for job entry or retraining" (Knapp 1981, p. 2). Since nearly all individuals will have to work in order to fulfill their needs, work has now become a right (Knapp).

With all the latest changes in the labor market, a number of adults looking for paid work for the first time do not always hold the degree that satisfies the requirements of a specific job (Cross; Marienau and Chickering). Because they have traditionally worked in the home or in volunteer organizations without pay, women are among those most affected by this situation (Ekstrom). It has been proven that skills acquired in the home by women can sometimes correspond to the skills of a paid job (Sharon; Ekstrom and Eliason; Schaeffer and Lynton). Women now want these skills to be officially recognized. Obtaining a degree allows women to better understand the worth of the learning they have acquired, which, in turn, improves their chances of getting a better job (Ekstrom; Rubin; Ray).

But women are not the only people who want to obtain a degree to maximize their chances of getting interesting and better-paying jobs. Ethnic minorities with different cultures and backgrounds (Gray and Davis) could benefit from prior learning assessment since most of them do not have official documents that attest their competence.

An academic degree is also a moral guarantee of competence (Ekstrom and others; Gray and Davis; Neff). Holding a degree means better chances for those who, for instance, have been the victims of their social status or cultural background (Stack and Hutton).

It seems, then, that the desire to get a degree is directly related to the possibility of a better job (Nickse; Chickering; Little). The degree is thus perceived as offering better chances for a job or promotion (Sharon; Ekstrom). Because of the numerous changes in the work place, including the ways in which jobs are performed, it is a fact of life today that workers have to retrain in order to adjust to the new or changing requirements of their jobs (Stack and Hutton; Matusak). It may indeed be that if their prior learning was assessed, workers would be more motivated to retrain since they would have at their disposal a profile of their present knowledge and could then learn what they lacked in order to become more competent in their job and perhaps eventually get a degree (Munce; Craig and Evers).

Unions strongly advocate a training and development program in conjunction with a prior learning assessment program. They have opened discussions with colleges and universities about developing programs that would offer their members the possibility of completing a training program and even obtaining a degree in their fields of specialization (Rosenstein and Stack).

While the primary reason adults give to have their prior learning assessed is to receive a degree in order to get a job, getting a job is not the only reason why adults would want to obtain an academic degree. Indeed, even those who already have stimulating careers and have attained their professional goals may want to have their learning assessed. When writing about people who want to have their learning assessed, Mark and Dewess remark: "Some of these people have often reached the top of their profession or have developed their own businesses and consequently do not need the certification or promotional possibilities that come with having a degree. . . . For many, the idea of earning a college degree is simply a personal desire" (Mark and Dewess 1984, p. 19). Some people want an academic degree because it serves as official proof of their learning and like the prestige and increased social status the degree brings. This reasoning can be explained by the fact that we live in a society that gives more and more importance to accreditation. Maehl writes: "We are a credentialed society and are likely to become more so rather than less so" (Maehl 1982, p. 38). As Maehl observes, the respect that society accords to a degree is so widespread that many adults wish to have their prior learning recognized in order to obtain a degree and the social status it brings (Maehl). Because society in general still regards a degree so highly, adults who get one consequently tend to feel a higher sense of accomplishment (Taylor). Prior learning assessment leading to accreditation represents, in the eyes of society, an adult's reward for working hard in his job and throughout his life (Rubin).

TO BRING MORE MEANING TO THEIR LIVES

Because of the fast pace of social change, people often find themselves modifying their ways of living. One unfortunate consequence of this is that people tend to lose the meaning they originally wanted for themselves and their lives. Time to think is scarce because adults are required to perform many tasks during one day. Today, within a 24-hour period, adults work, play, and study day, night, and even on weekends (Burley; Chickering; Cross; Keeton and Tate). These facts of daily life seem to create some confusion as to what adults want for themselves (McClure; Singer). Adults simultaneously experience several different kinds of experiences and they question the nature of their needs, their values, who they are, and what they want to become.

Adults are afraid of losing control over their lives (Community Colleges of Vermont), and so would like to be sure that they will keep control of their own lives and give their lives the meaning they want (Community Colleges of Vermont; Shulman; Marienau and Chickering; Rosenman; Ray). Adults are more and more aware in these times of rapid change of the importance to live the way they want in agreement with their fundamental and developmental needs (Marienau and Chickering). They want to live fully, day after day (Presno), giving priority to their personal and social values (Axelrod; Greenberg).

Moreover, adults would like to be able to turn to the academic milieu to build their life plan, considering all the activities motivating them to adjust to change (Chickering). Watkins writes that adults would like institutions to help them build a life project (Watkins).

To summarize, adults have to satisfy their fundamental and developmental needs, and to do so, they must find new ways to adapt to change. Therefore, they believe that it is only fair that schools assess their learning to help them continue this learning process, thereby enabling them to obtain an academic degree, with all its intrinsic advantages, and live a meaningful life.

REASONS FOR ACADEMIC INSTITUTIONS TO ASSESS PRIOR LEARNING

Academic institutions receiving requests from adults for prior learning assessment have their own set of fundamental and developmental needs to satisfy. The main reasons given in the literature to justify the implementation of a prior learning assessment program in an academic institution are to guarantee the reliability and validity of the accreditation, to improve the institution's financial situation and to bring a new challenge to the faculty.

GUARANTEEING THE RELIABILITY AND VALIDITY OF THE ACCREDITATION

In our changing world, schools are no longer the only places where it is possible to acquire knowledge that is of an academic level. The home, often considered the first place where learning occurs (Smythe; Lamdin), gives many homemakers the possibility to acquire skills of a caliber equal to what is taught in schools (Ekstrom and Lockheed; Beier and Ekstrom; Schaeffer and Lynton). Volunteer associations have also become a place of learning and many teach their members various skills of academic value. For example, because of the greater importance attributed to volunteer work, the Red Cross reassessed the content and the outcomes of their training programs (Stoel). Because of the quality of some of the programs offered by volunteer associations, the U.S. federal government and the governments of individual states are now considering volunteer work in their admission test for the civil service (Reichlin).

The quality of the learning volunteers acquire in their work and training leads a number of authors to consider volunteers professionals in the same way that paid workers are, the only difference between the two groups being that the second group receives a salary for their work (Straus; Beier and Ekstrom; Rehnborg; Thornton; Reichlin; Ray; Stoel).

In assessing prior learning acquired through volunteer work and other ways, academic institutions would not only be fair to adults (Sharon), but they would allow the community to benefit from more services. This is because knowing that their services could be recognized, volunteers would be more motivated to serve the community (Lauffer and Gorodezky; O'Connell).

More and more employers offer on-the-job training through workshops and seminars. They give their employees and even top executives time to think (Cross). The business world and governments encourage their employees to seek advanced-level training to improve their performance (Sharon; Kruh). The quality of teaching or training given by these providers of education is very often equal to the quality of the training given in traditional schools (Hatala).

Unions have developed training programs for their members that suit their specific interests (Stack and Hutton).

Traditional institutions do offer courses and training programs to a clientele who wish to study in order to satisfy a variety of needs and interests that do not necessarily lead to a specific academic degree. Some institutions offer Continuing Education Units (CEU) that are recognized by some corporate and professional associations, as well as by government agencies and the military. However, these continuing education credits do not always correspond to the traditional credits given to students following courses in traditional programs (Goerke).

Each provider of education, whether it be a union, a volunteer organization, or an employer, has developed its own way of assessing the quality of the learning it teaches. Because of their large number and because the learning content varies, it is difficult to imagine a standard evaluation criteria for all. Therefore, judging the learning outcomes is far from easy (Gould). According to Martorana and Kuhns, academic institutions still hold the mandate to assess learning; consequently, the validity and reliability of accreditation should normally come under their authority.

Employers trust the validity and reliability of the accreditation awarded by academic institutions. That is why they ask that credits be recognized for their employees so that the employees can seek training only for what they do not know and have the possibility of completing a degree while keeping their full-time jobs (Strange).

Professional associations have their own requirements regarding the practice of their specialization (Hatala). They too expect the educational milieu to guarantee the validity and reliability of the knowledge acquired by their newly-graduated members (Hogan).

Academic institutions wishing to take on the responsibility of assessing the value of learning achieved outside their walls have to redefine their standards to ensure first, that they are being fair to the adults who approach them and second, that what they do corresponds to the ethical and moral criteria of which they are the guarantors (Central Michigan University; Keeton; Stanley).

IMPROVING THEIR FINANCIAL SITUATION

Another reason why academic institutions would engage in prior learning assessment is to improve their financial situation (Strange). For a number of years, the American economy was relatively good, particularly during the sixties and early seventies (Silverman and Tate). This allowed academic institutions to create new faculty, administrative, professional, and support jobs. During those years, rapid promotion, tenure, sabbaticals and retirement benefits were the norm. New buildings sprang up everywhere, and new and sophisticated equipment was purchased for large amounts of money.

By the end of the seventies and at the beginning of the eighties, the economy in higher education changed (Goldstein; Gold). Academic institutions now find themselves competing with each other to attract or even keep their student clientele. In addition, academic institutions now have to compete with unions, employers, government agencies, hospitals, military services and professional associations (Hatala). Student recruitment by all these competitors provoked a lowering of the student clientele for academic institutions (Kruh). A smaller clientele means smaller revenues for academic institutions who still must pay the long-term mortgages they acquired during the years of prosperity (Silverman and Tate).

Business and industry have developed their own computer programs without the help and leadership of academic institutions (Matusak; Lynton; Hatala; Jacobs). So, because of their new expertise, employers are now in a position to teach as well as schools.

In 1979, the American Society for Training and Development conducted a survey that revealed that the annual education budget in the business environment exceeds 30 billion dollars (Craig and Evers). This amount has now doubled, and the actual budget spent for learning and training outside of school approximates that of colleges and universities. *Harper's* magazine gives the following statistics: "Total annual expenditures of U.S. corporations on employee-education programs: $60,000,000,000. Total annual expenditures of U.S. four-year public and private colleges/universities: $60,000,000,000" (Harper's, April 1985).

Teaching and training, which were until recently the exclusive concern of academic institutions, are now out in the business world. Cross predicted in 1978 that by the 21st century, sophisticated technology and easy communication would modify the place of learning and turn the world into a large campus.

Today, academic institutions are faced with budget cuts and a reduction in government grants (Greenberg) that have limited the number of new projects they can take on (Bushnell). At the same time as the grants for academic institutions are going down (Knapp), the cost of education is going up. That is why academic institutions are now seeking new solutions to keep professors and teachers in their jobs occupying classrooms and using the equipment in which academic institutions have invested so much.

Because the prior learning assessment program does attract a new clientele, academic institutions could put all of their expensive resources to good use. It might compensate for the loss of revenue resulting from the decrease in young students attending their institutions (Stanley; Matusak; Heeger). Moreover, a new clientele would allow institutions to receive the grants they are accustomed to obtaining (Witkowski).

Academic institutions see in prior learning assessment the possibility to develop a new market (Cross). Some of this new market would be composed of workers and union members wishing to return to school (Levine and Hutton; Stack and Hutton; Stack and Paskal). Craig and Evers believe that higher education could increase its market if the needs of workers could be better evaluated. Academic institutions realize the potential of an adult clientele in terms of their numbers and the added revenue they could bring (Smith).

Several academic institutions believe that by recognizing prior learning, the money they already have would be put to better use because adults would acquire complementary knowledge instead of repeating courses on subjects that they already master (Eliason; McGarraghy and Reilly).

In conclusion, the financial problems of academic institutions cannot be taken lightly and it would appear that prior learning assessment offers a way to alleviate them (Matusak).

PROVIDING TEACHERS AND PROFESSORS WITH A NEW CHALLENGE

In the past, the expectations society had for a professor or teacher was that he be a good speaker, an active learner, and able to develop new courses. His contribution to society was the result of these accomplishments.

Times have changed. Today's society expects a lot more from professors and teachers: they must reassess and redefine their roles in education and outside the academic milieu (Bradley and Bolman). They must cope with new and ongoing challenges and still satisfy the ethical and moral standards guaranteed by schools (Cross). More than ever, teachers have become the agents of change in a society that is itself constantly changing (Martorana and Kuhns; Wolfe; Mauksch).

Administrators at academic institutions realize that the changes professors must experience may cause some to lose part of their primary motivation for their chosen work: to teach and judge the quality of learning. The recognition of prior learning can be a way to give them a new challenge to overcome this lack of motivation (Taylor), especially if they are guaranteed the role of experts in the assessment of the prior learning (Matusak).

Assessing prior learning gives teachers the opportunity to judge for themselves the quality of the learning linked to their fields of competence that has been acquired outside of school, using the assessment method of their choice (Bradley and Bolman). Moreover, working in the field of prior learning assessment gives teachers the opportunity to teach and assess the skills of an adult student clientele, a clientele that is very often more motivated to learn than their younger counterparts (Mahoney).

When they assess prior learning, teachers evaluate learning outcomes in a new way, regardless of whether the learning is in the cognitive or affective domain. Loacker and Palola write: "Faculty concern for what students learn becomes a definite commitment to making learning results—both cognitive and affective—explicit and to evaluating that learning with appropriate instruments" (Loacker and Palola 1981, p. viii). Prior learning assessment allows the teaching faculty to become more familiar with the characteristics of adults and with the various different contexts in which they learn. This, in turn, allows teachers to make progress in the field of adult education. Menson writes that "only as adult educators begin to think about various contexts within which their learning takes place will the profession of adult education advance" (Menson 1982*b*, p. 117).

When they are helping adults in the process of prior learning assessment, teachers work differently from the way they usually work with younger students. They also undergo important changes that allow them to focus on their own objectives and make new discoveries about themselves. Krueger writes: "It seems that in the process of helping students to solidify their goals, faculty members have discovered things about themselves and their own goals" (Krueger 1982, p. 97).

Working in the field of prior learning assessment allows professors to become aware of the new needs of adults, and at the same time, they find themselves assuming the roles of intellectual leaders and political and cultural advisers (Keeton).

From this systematic analysis of the main subjects discussed in the literature emerges the underlying ideological principles of prior learning assessment. They are summarized below.

IDEOLOGICAL PRINCIPLES OF PRIOR LEARNING ASSESSMENT

There is abundant evidence in the prior learning assessment literature of the great deal of respect the writers have for adults. Esteemed as individuals who have their own identities, adults are regarded as having the right to learn by building on the basis of what they know already, and to live in the way that best suits them.

Many authors specialized in the field of prior learning assessment really put themselves in the position of the adults they study, defending their interests and writing on their behalf. Through their research, these authors enable others to understand the nature, needs, evolution and aspirations of adults or groups of adults who have acquired specific learning at some point of their lives in a variety of contexts.

Prior learning assessment is a modern phenomenon that is directly related to the needs of adults regardless of their age, sex, ethnic origin or social status. This phenomenon is also related to the needs of academic institutions, whatever their specialization, educational objectives or operational procedures.

Adults have the responsibility to continue to learn throughout their lives in order that they may satisfy their fundamental and developmental needs and lead better, more fulfilling lives in consequence. Academic institutions share this responsibility to learn. For their part, they must learn to help adults identify the learning they have acquired that is of academic value.

Furthermore, institutions must learn to subsequently assess and accredit the newly-identified learning.

Prior learning assessment is built on the following principles: *justice* and *equity, ethics* and *morals* and, finally, *responsibility*. What exactly do these values mean? They are explained below with the help of the dictionary of philosophical terms by André Lalande, entitled *Vocabulaire technique et critique de la philosophie* (Technical and Critical Vocabulary of Philosophy).

The word *justice* comes from the word "just," which means to conform to a right, whether it be natural or positive. The word *equity* signifies a sure and spontaneous feeling of what is just and unjust, usually in respect to a concrete situation.

Adults see in prior learning assessment a way in which academic institutions can accord them the respect they deserve as individuals and do justice to the new learning they have acquired as members of a society that is undergoing rapid change and modifying their needs. Prior learning assessment, then, provides institutions with a concrete way to show their respect of the individual and his learning by a fair and just assessment of the learning. This allows adults to attain their goals of obtaining an academic degree and bringing new meaning to their lives more rapidly.

Like their new adult clientele, academic institutions too must live with change and fulfill their own specific needs at the same time. Prior learning assessment gives to educational institutions the right to do justice to the quality of an individual's learning and evaluate this learning while at the same time ensuring the validity and reliability of the accreditation they give. Prior learning assessment also gives institutions the opportunity to satisfy such needs as improving their financial situation and providing their faculty with a new challenge.

Lalande defines *ethics* as the science whose objective is to judge and appreciate the distinction between good and bad.

Morals are defined as the established rules of conduct that are considered unconditionally valid.

Prior learning assessment requires institutions to respond to the fundamental and developmental needs of adults by judging, with rigor and consistency, the quality of the learning outcomes with respect to preestablished academic requirements, using methods whose validity and reliability cannot be questioned.

A person with a sense of *responsibility* is one who is accountable for his actions and will not attempt to deal out the responsibility to someone else. A person who possesses moral responsibility is aware of the consequences of his actions.

When they request to have their prior learning assessed, adults take on the responsibility of going through the process of having to prove their learning. Academic institutions who make the decision to assess prior learning also have a responsibility. They have the responsibility to validate the knowledge already acquired by adults by making just and fair decisions about the nature of their learning. These judgments must be in conformity with the established rules of ethics and morals in practice at the academic institution. The quality of the judgment rendered will be related to the particular method used to assess the prior learning.

These principles of justice and equity are meant for adults who ask academic institutions to recognize their right to satisfy their fundamental needs and develop in a changing society. They demand justice and equity so that they can obtain a degree, which, in turn, will help them to obtain a job, further their training or improve their social status. Adults also want to bring meaning to their lives in a constantly-changing world.

When they respond to the request of adults to assess their prior learning, educational institutions can also respond to their own fundamental and developmental needs both fairly and equitably. They can guarantee the reliability and validity of the prior learning accreditation process, improve their financial situation and give their faculty a new challenge.

Adults want educational institutions to develop methods to assess prior learning that are unquestionably valid and reliable so that their learning will be considered as valid as the learning acquired by younger students. For their part, educational institutions want to fulfill their new mandate by rigorously honoring their principles of ethics and morals to ensure that the credits obtained through prior learning assessment will have the same credibility as those obtained the traditional way.

Adults have the responsibility to ask schools for help and it is up to adults to prove the quality of their learning. The academic institution has the responsibility to help an adult to prove what he knows, and make a judgment on this prior learning that is in conformity with the principles of justice and equity, ethics and morals and, finally, give proper accreditation for the learning so that the adult may further his learning if necessary.

In this way, both principal partners, the adult and the academic institution, can satisfy their own fundamental and developmental needs in a society characterized by change.

CHAPTER

Methodological Principles

CHAPTER 3

Methodological Principles

Chapter 3 identifies the methodological principles on which prior learning assessment is founded. As explained in Chapter 1, these as well as the ideological principles are not identified explicitly in the literature. The prior learning assessment literature describes a number of different methods used to assess prior learning. This study has set out to discover which methods are most frequently used in the United States and whether these frequently used methods include the entire process of prior learning recognition as defined by Spille, that is, the identification, assessment and accreditation of experiential learning. Spille's definition describes the main stages in the prior learning assessment process. This study examines the various operations at each stage of the process in an attempt to identify the fundamental methodological principles.

The three most frequently used methods to recognize prior learning in the United States are: standardized tests, credit recommendations and individual evaluations.

The standardized tests used in the United States are exams like those in the College Level Examination Program (CLEP), for example, which are created by a team of specialists from different disciplines. The tests usually consist of multiple-choice questions.

Credit recommendations are made by teams of professors specialized in a particular discipline that assess the competence of teachers at a non-academic institution and analyze the course contents. Once the quality of the course and the competence of the teachers have been established, the non-academic organization receives accreditation. From then on, adults who successfully complete courses in the accredited non-academic institution have the opportunity to see their learning officially recognized by traditional academic institutions. The credit recommendations most often referred to in the literature are those made by the American Council on Education (ACE).

Tests and credit recommendations are very close to the traditional ways in which learning is assessed. However, these methods do not do justice to adults and their learning. For example, often standardized tests allow the adult to show some, but not all of the learning he has acquired. Thus Reilly writes: "Standardized tests, for example, are usually inadequate or inappropriate" (Reilly and others 1977, p. v). And unfortunately, credit recommendations are not always accepted by traditional academic institutions.

At the time when they return to school, adults may have acquired learning that is quite diverse in nature. The learning may be related to a number of different disciplines and be at different academic levels. The varied nature of the learning creates new problems for faculty and administrators, as Reilly observes: "The individualized and often highly unique nature of experiential learning poses a number of problems for the faculty members and administrators charged with the assessment of that learning" (Reilly and others 1977, p. v). Therefore, the literature stresses the necessity for a method of assessment that can appreciate the specific experiential learning of each adult, a method that can allow others to judge the learning fairly (Hodgkinson). The individualized method most referred to in the literature is called the *portfolio method.*

The portfolio method or program, as it is often called in the literature, has evolved over the years and has influenced the entire process of prior learning assessment. In 1976, the portfolio program was described in eight steps by Fremer. That same year, Willingham and Geisinger developed a 13-stage process for portfolio development. This second model has been used by a large number of institutions that are members of CAEL. Not long after he elaborated his portfolio program, Willingham stressed the importance of paying particular attention to the management and coordination of the program. This is necessary because of the way the program forces institutions to rethink their traditional way of judging and functioning (Keeton).

Over the years the portfolio method has undergone a number of modifications (Knapp and Gardiner) and today it is acclaimed as the method *par excellence* to recognize and assess prior learning (Knapp; Forrest). Because the portfolio is the method most discussed in the literature, it is the method used here to understand the entire process of prior learning assessment.

This study uses Willingham and Geisinger's model of the portfolio method as it was adapted by Cantin in the third chapter of a report of the evaluation committee on St. Félicien's experience of prior learning assessment in nursing *(Rapport du Comité d'évaluation de l'expérience de St-Félicien concernant la reconnaissance des acquis en techniques infirmières)*. Cantin regroups in one phase all the elements related to the planning of the prior learning assessment process. The other steps are those found in the definition of the prior learning process, that is, the identification, assessment and accreditation of learning.

In addition to describing the importance of identifying, assessing and accrediting learning, the literature makes repeated mention of the importance of planning the prior learning assessment process. Each step, from the planning stage to the accrediting stage, involves different operations and they are described below.

This study has found that the same procedures keep coming up in the prior learning assessment literature to describe the different operations of each stage. Once all of the stages and the operations have been identified and explained, it is possible to identify the methodological principles of prior learning assessment.

PLANNING THE PROGRAM

As has been discussed in the previous chapter, both adults and academic institutions have to satisfy their needs of maintenance and development in a society that is constantly changing. How is it possible, though, for an institution to satisfy its own needs and at the same time those of adults, all the while respecting the ideological principles of prior learning assessment?

The literature unanimously recommends meticulous planning of all the operations in the prior learning assessment process to avoid allowing the process to become a cheap and compromised process of accreditation. Keeton cautions: "A watch must be kept out for degree mills, 'rip-offs,' and well-intentioned but poorly managed educational programs" (Keeton 1978, p. 37). As Stanley notes, careful planning of the prior learning assessment process assures its quality (Stanley).

The literature was consulted to discover what, according to most writers, is the best way to implement a prior learning assessment program. The planning process described in this study is based on the rules established by Willingham. Willingham's rules have inspired many institutions; they use his rules either as they are or adapt them to their specific needs.

As the literature notes, the planning stage begins with the administrators, who have to engage in careful study before they can implement a prior learning assessment procedure.

REASONS AND MOTIVES

Once administrators have decided to implement a prior learning assessment program, they must examine their reasons or motivations for doing so (Willingham; Shulman; Martorana and Kuhns). These reasons may vary. Some institutions, for example, would like to answer students' needs, while others would do so because they want to attract a new clientele in order to keep or maintain faculty jobs. Some institutions might decide to recognize prior learning because they want to offer equal opportunities to women and minorities in their area (Beier and Ekstrom); others might seek to fulfill a social mandate (Hatala). Whatever their reasons, planners should not put economic considerations at the forefront of their decision to recognize prior learning since the primary mission of any academic institution should be first and foremost education (Sachs).

CHARACTERISTICS OF THE PROGRAM

Prior learning assessment programs may vary slightly in their application from one institution to another, but the general characteristics of the programs are comparable in all institutions (Sachs). These general characteristics are related to the administration and coordination of the program, its scope and duration, the material and human resources required, the educational objectives, and the expected outcomes.

MANAGING AND COORDINATING THE PROGRAM

Once administrators have agreed on their reasons or motives to offer a prior learning assessment program, they must inform the teaching staff and other interested professionals of their intentions and subsequently create a planning committee. The planning committee would be composed of the people who will participate in the prior learning assessment program once it gets underway. These include the academic dean, the counselors who will eventually help the students (Ekstrom) and professors who will assess the learning outcomes (O'Connell; Sachs; Heermann and others). The planning committee's principal task is to develop the procedures for the prior learning assessment program (Willingham).

Once the planning has been done and each operation in the prior learning assessment program has been rigorously studied, the planning committee could pass the responsibility for the day-to-day management and coordination of the program to another administrative body in the institution (Sachs).

SCOPE OF THE PROGRAM

The members of the planning committee must decide on how extensive their prior learning assessment program will be. To do so, the committee will need to closely examine the particular situation at their institution. A number of different factors, such as the institution's geographic location and its particular priorities

(MacTaggart) can have an impact on the first prior learning experiment it undertakes.

The institution may decide to begin its prior learning assessment program with a homogeneous group of adults of roughly the same age and cultural background, or a group of adults who have worked in the same field—volunteers, for example (Taylor). An institution's first prior learning assessment experiment could be run as a pilot project (MacTaggart and Knapp).

During the planning stage, it is advisable to fix a quota on the number of students admitted to the program because institutions run the risk of having too many students, given the popularity of the program. The literature does not specify the number of students institutions should initially limit themselves to. Nevertheless, it appears that institutions usually admit only small groups of between 8 to 10 students (Schatz and others) in the course on portfolio development, with 15 students being the maximum (Heermann and others).

Judging from the rapid growth of the prior learning assessment program at Webster College in St. Louis, Missouri, where the clientele increased by up to 345% in the six-year period between 1978 and 1983 (Fugate and MacTaggart), the planners should anticipate a rapid growth in their program and be prepared to welcome many new adult students.

The planners must also decide what sorts of educational programs can accommodate the prior learning credits. These may be certificate or undergraduate programs, for example. In the United States, it seems that the first-cycle program, which leads to a bachelor's degree, is the program in which most adults normally register and request to have their learning officially recognized (Strange).

The program planners should anticipate that adults may request to pursue independent studies (Dwyer and Torgoff; Stanley) and institutions should be willing to draw up learning contracts for this purpose (Warren and Breen; Mahoney; Knapp and Gardiner).

DURATION OF THE PROGRAM

According to the literature, the optimal duration of a prior learning assessment program is two semesters (Fugate and MacTaggart) because adults need at least one semester to reflect on their prior learning and collect all the relevant data and another semester to have the prior learning assessed (Rydell).

MATERIAL RESOURCES

Equipment, classrooms and other materials normally used for students in traditional programs might be used for the new adult clientele in the prior learning assessment program as well (Stanley; Matusak; Heeger). Markovich and Malling suggest that institutions explore the possibilities offered by computer resources, particularly in seminars on portfolio development.

EDUCATIONAL OBJECTIVES

The planning committee must help adults in the prior learning program attain their educational projects (Lamdin) by assigning as much importance to their learning objectives as they do to those of traditional students (Proffitt and Di Spirito).

Planners could question the educational value of the prior learning assessment process (Rydell) and the link between the proposed educational objectives and the experience adults have acquired prior to registering in the program (Shulman; Hatala). In this way, adults would then be able to study using their strengths rather than their weaknesses. Thus Taylor writes of "meeting students at the point of their strength of preparation, rather than, as is too often the case, at the point of their academic weaknesses" (Taylor 1982*b*, p. 6).

Planners of the prior learning assessment program also need to verify that with the educational objectives they propose, which include cognitive development, sensitivity, emotional and moral development and practical skills in specific fields, the planned program does not encourage the improvement of certain skills while precluding adults from experiencing immediate satisfaction and taking pleasure in studying and living (Keeton).

EXPECTED OUTCOMES

For adults, some of the possible outcomes of their participation in a prior learning assessment program are the satisfaction of their maintenance and developmental needs (Fugate and Mac-Taggart) and a reduction in the time and money they spend on their studies (Ekstrom; Ekstrom and others; Jamison and Wolfe; Avakian and Lipsett; Hogan; Warren; Shipton and Steltenpohl; Heermann and others; Knapp).

For institutions, the potential outcomes are many. In addition to gradually satisfying the institution's maintenance and developmental needs as described above, the prior learning program will bring institutions a much larger mature student clientele with a wide variety of acquired learning (Cross; Maehl). This new adult clientele could include a great number of volunteers (Beier and Ekstrom; Ekstrom; Reichlin; Ray), unionized workers (Stack and Paskal), and adults at a mid-life transition stage (Menson). Adults who already possess an academic degree and have practical experience in their chosen profession may also enroll in the program because of the new, complementary learning they acquire each year as a result of the rapid changes taking place in their profession and/or the society in which they live. This is true of medical doctors, for example (Goerke). This program could help women by increasing their chances to find a job (Beier and Ekstrom; Schaeffer and Lynton).

Another outcome for institutions with prior learning assessment programs will be the new role they will have with respect to the business community and professional organizations. Employers and non-profit organizations will approach institutions that provide prior learning assessment for help with the training and development of their staff and members (Strange). Professional associations may also ask for help to review their standards of professional practice and to create other methods to define the competence of their members (Hogan).

Institutions can anticipate that the degrees they eventually grant to their new adult clientele will build competence in a specific discipline within the community (Klemp; Wolfe; Olson).

COUNSELLING SERVICES FOR STUDENTS

In the prior learning assessment literature, the responsibility to assist students usually rests with qualified counselors (advisers, mentors, student advocates and sometimes andragogical counselors—counselors specialized in dealing with adults) and members of the teaching staff (Ekstrom). The counselors would help students from the time they seek admission to the institution (Klemp) and throughout the development of their portfolio (Haines and Schwoebel). The teaching faculty would have to both counsel the students and evaluate the results of their acquired learning (Preston).

The planners of the prior learning assessment program can expect to hold seminars and courses to help students to better understand the process they are about to undertake. The courses and seminars will undoubtedly improve students' chances of having their learning recognized (Stanley; Fisher-Thompson; Warren and Breen; Rydell).

HUMAN RESOURCES

The human resources required for a prior learning assessment program are identical to those required for any other educational program. However, because prior learning assessment is concerned primarily with adults, the human resources for the program should be selected according to their knowledge of adults and their needs (Willingham and Geisinger). Since institutions already have counselors to help younger students, this same service should be extended to adults (Fugate and MacTaggart).

DEVELOPING AND ORGANIZING THE HUMAN RESOURCES

The second operation in the planning stage is to develop and organize the human resources. From the literature, it is possible to isolate three main tasks in this operation: selecting competent and motivated individuals, identifying each person's tasks, and planning professional development courses and seminars.

SELECTING THE PRIOR LEARNING PERSONNEL

The administrators of the prior learning assessment program should be chosen by the program director, the dean, or, in the case of assessors, by the department heads (Stanley).

The counselors could be chosen from among the counselors or teaching staff already in place. Those selected would be known for the quality of their relationship with adults (McIntyre).

The assessors would normally be recruited from among the regular teaching staff of the institution. Several writers point out that well-chosen evaluators will be one of the strengths of the program (Christensen; Kray). The planners of the prior learning assessment program must look for assessors who have good general skills and an intuition for detail. The ideal assessor must have the motivation, employment stability and experience that enables him to defend and promote the program, especially when confronted with budget restrictions (McIntyre).

Planners could seek out professors who teach in the discipline of the learning to be assessed or a permanent committee composed of professors from different disciplines and, if need be, outside experts, former graduates and adult students to conduct the assessments (Stanley). Assessors will also be chosen from among experts, that is, people who have acquired specific skills through experience, education or training (Reilly). The assessors will be required to demonstrate their skills in other domains because of the different roles they will be called upon to play in the program (McIntyre).

The program planners must verify the qualifications and training of all those approached to act as assessors of prior learning (Willingham and Geisinger; Fremer). They will choose individuals who are acknowledged for the quality of their judgment in order to ensure that all students will be treated with fairness. On this subject, Reilly writes: "Competent judges . . . can ensure an equitable and consistent treatment of all students" (Reilly and others 1977, p. 1). The evaluators must not only be competent in the field of learning to be evaluated, they must be very good judges. Indeed, the quality and integrity of the assessor's judgment is supremely important. Reilly writes: "It is especially important, then, that the assessors, in addition to being experts in a particular substantive domain, also be competent judges. Experts who are not properly prepared to conduct assessments jeopardize the equity of assessment for the institution and more importantly, for the individual student" (Reilly and others 1977, p. 1).

TASKS OF THE ADMINISTRATORS, COUNSELORS AND ASSESSORS

Each of the three principal participants in the prior learning assessment program, the administrators, counselors and assessors, has a specific set of tasks to perform.

Tasks of the Administrators

The main task of the administrators is to ensure the establishment and smooth operation of the prior learning assessment program.

They will have to be prepared to face resistance to the program from some people, particularly teachers. Often this resistance is due to insufficient or erroneous information. Professors who tend to resist the establishment of a prior learning assessment program do so out of fear that lower standards of evaluation will creep in or that they will be identified as accreditation and evaluation agents (Kray). Planners of the prior learning program can expect that professors will question them about their working conditions and the quality of the standards of the institution. Professors will also want guarantees that the institution will not give away credits for life experiences as such (Knapp). Some teachers might be resistant to the prior learning assessment program (McIntyre) simply because they do not feel adequately prepared to make the necessary changes to deal with older students (Preston). Some professors may think that recognizing experiential learning is not a very rigorous way to credit learning and that, in consequence, the quality of the regular programs offered by the institutions will be threatened (Stanley; Knapp). Those who plan the prior learning program can also expect that teachers will fear losing their jobs or being assigned to other duties (Avakian and Lipsett; Evans and others) because they associate the recognition of prior learning with a reduction in the number of courses they teach. Stanley writes: "Critics also express the concern that faculty members will be displaced if students receive credit through evaluation instead of through classroom participation" (Stanley 1980, p. 24). A final worry is the loss of prestige for an institution and a reduction in the regular clientele (MacTaggart).

These attitudes can be explained by the fact that in some institutions, professors have never heard about credits given for experiential learning, while in other institutions, misinformed professors are still wondering if it is a good idea to grant credits for learning that is experiential (Knapp).

Given the resistance professors can have to the prior learning assessment program, there is an obvious need to apply some quality control to the program in order to guarantee that the institutions' standards are maintained (Stanley).

Administrators, then, have the duty to ensure that those who hold key responsibilities within the prior learning assessment program (like teachers) will be given proper training on their future roles and tasks (Willingham).

Tasks of the Counselors

The counselors will have to provide assistance particularly during the time when adults identify their learning outcomes (Mahoney). A large number of adults have acquired important and valuable experience in the business world or in community work, while others have completed studies that have been credited at other institutions (Fugate and MacTaggart).

The counselor must help adults to develop as individuals (Chickering; Matusak; Knapp and Gardiner) and help them to persevere, especially when developing their portfolios (Mahoney).

Counselors must help adults to acquire more confidence in themselves, and since many adults may not have attended an academic institution for quite some time, counselors should help adults to understand the requirements of academic institutions (Mark and Menson; Thomas and others). Counselors would also be the ones to demystify the fears that some adults have with respect to their age (Cross; Menson; Mahoney). Counselors may also be called upon to verify the basic skills of adults in reading, writing and mathematics (Rydell).

Counselors or professors who are given the responsibility to teach the course on portfolio development have a number of possible additional tasks to perform. To begin, they must have good listening skills and be ready to teach writing/editing skills, make an early evaluation of the competence of their students, and be attentive to their students' needs, giving them the support they need (Nickse).

Tasks of the Assessors

The principal evaluators will be teachers whose main task is to assess the skills that are relevant to their particular discipline (Willingham).

Because the assessment process can involve professors from different departments, planners should prepare for the creation of an interdisciplinary committee to oversee the evaluation process. Such a committee would allow teachers to work together to reach an agreement on the learning outcomes to be assessed (Sachs).

The main task of an assessor is to measure the nature, quality and extent of the learning, and finally, to assess that learning using established criteria (Reilly; Willingham).

FACULTY DEVELOPMENT

Very often in a university, the faculty members and counselors already hold a doctoral degree and are recognized authorities in a specific discipline. People expect these individuals, especially professors, to know how to teach and evaluate the knowledge acquired by their students. Assessments are made from predicted results. For example, a psychology professor creates a course and teaches it to his students, prepares exams on the subject and expects his students to answer the exam questions in a specific way.

Given the fact that prior learning assessment is a new field, professors, counselors and administrators would undoubtedly benefit from professional development even before the service to assess prior learning is offered (McIntyre; MacTaggart and Knapp) and periodic professional development sessions once the program has begun (MacTaggart and Knapp).

Actually, all those involved in the prior learning assessment program could benefit from professional development in order to ensure that they perform their new tasks well. Whitaker writes: "All of us need more training in the assessment of learning—wherever, whenever, and however it occurs" (Whitaker 1978, p. 68). Following the example of the institutional members of CAEL who recognize the importance of professional development, planners should regard the proper training of the professors, who will be the judges of the experiential learning, as the key to the success of the entire program (Knapp). Consequently, it becomes essential to offer professors a professional development program (Menson; McIntyre; Mahoney).

The professional development program could be designed using an andragogical approach, as Knowles advocates, to help administrators, counselors and assessors to fulfill their responsibilities (Henderson and Hyre; Shipton and Steltenpohl). This training would enable all those involved in the prior learning assessment program to move from pedagogy to andragogy, which would favor the establishment of a new relationship between educators and adult students. Allen writes: "A shift from pedagogy to 'andragogy' is suggested by advocates like Knowles . . . to emphasize the need for a new, more mature relationship between graduate educators and experienced adult learners" (Allen and Jacobs 1982, p. 69). When discussing the development program, McIntyre suggests the use of self-evaluation methods (the "self-diagnostic rating scale," Knowles) to better evaluate the competence of the professors.

Planners of the professional development program should also aim for an increase in the knowledge and understanding of the development and needs of adults, using the theories of Knowles, Erickson, Chickering and Dewey, all of which insist on the role of experience, the liberty to choose and the responsibility adults will take for the consequences that follow from the choices they make (Cross).

Since prior learning assessment would be made mostly through the portfolio method, counselors and professors would be invited to develop their own portfolios before asking students to do the same. This is confirmed by Withorn and Cedrone when they write: "What emerges here is that we need to do what we so often require of our students: prepare portfolios" (Withorn and Cedrone 1979, p. 67). Once the counselors and professors have completed their own portfolios, their professional development programs can concentrate on themes related to adult education and on the assessment of prior learning (McIntyre).

All those who favor institutional changes need to understand human development (Marienau and Chickering; Overly and others; Menson). Administrators, counselors and assessors could think of ways in which they could better integrate adult students into their intellectual world (Lamdin).

A professional development program could cover subjects ranging from evaluating learning, teaching the course on portfolio development, using counselling techniques, and understanding different learning styles, how adults develop, and experiential learning as such (Mahoney).

ADMISSION RULES AND REQUIREMENTS

This study found that where admission rules are concerned, institutions apply criteria for adults that are different from those they apply to younger students and the admission criteria for adults can vary considerably from one institution to the next.

The planners of the prior learning assessment program can expect students with credits or credit recommendations from other traditional institutions to come seeking prior learning recognition (Hatala). Some of these students may already have a high school diploma (or equivalent), while others without a diploma might nevertheless display an acceptable level of reading and writing skills (Kelly; "entry-level skill proficiency," Nickse).

When planners review their admission rules, they could decide to admit only those students who have an obvious chance of receiving credits. Keeton writes: "To be realistic about its choice of priorities for quality, an institution should systematically study the entering qualifications and achievements of its learners" (Keeton 1980, p. 96).

The Behavioral Event Interview developed by David McLelland could also be used as a method for selecting students for admission. This interview, which uses behaviorist theories, would be a means to evaluate the level of a person's knowledge (Klemp).

Admission could also be limited to older students who have already completed part of their educational program, for example (MacTaggart and Knapp).

Institutions considering implementing a prior learning assessment program may want to follow the example of Webster's Center of Individual and Professional Development located in St. Louis, Missouri, which offers preadmission counselling for its students. Each potential student must write a detailed description of his life and work experiences that are related to a specific academic level. Once this summary has been reviewed by a counselor, the student is interviewed to determine if he can eventually have his skills assessed by a committee. If the outcome of this interview is favorable, the student can choose to register in the course on portfolio development (Fugate and MacTaggart).

TYPE OF CLIENTELE

While the prior learning assessment literature does not give information on the age of the clients enrolled in the prior learning assessment programs, planners can expect an older clientele that is more concerned about their educational development (O'Connell). The clientele that benefits most from prior learning assessment in higher education usually seems to be from the middle class (Menson).

A difference in the age group of the registering population can be expected, depending on the institution and the region where the planners are creating their prior learning assessment program. For example, the typical student at Adelphi University was between 30 and 40 years old, had a good deal of experience in the business world or in community work and had already acquired credits from other colleges or universities (Fugate and MacTaggart). At Sinclair Community College in Ohio, the typical student was 40 years old and had a good deal of knowledge acquired through paid employment or in the business world for the most part (Fugate and MacTaggart).

Program planners should expect to count on having a large number of women who have either been homemakers or volunteers among their new clientele (Ekstrom). Many of these women return to school with a new perception of their role and wish to study for a particular career (Lapine and Moore).

DEFINING STUDENTS' PERFORMANCE CRITERIA

The performance criteria expected of students must also be established and these criteria must be taken into consideration at the time the experiential learning is assessed (Nickse). The performance criteria established will depend on the educational program and encourage the attainment of new educational objectives (Warren).

The student performance criteria can be established with respect to the following: the development of the student's personal objectives, the basic educational mission and objectives of the institution or the department concerned and finally, the requirements established from outside the institution (Fremer) by employers, for example.

Prior learning assessment will be restricted to the learning that corresponds to a minimum of academic requirements (Maehl). Those planning the prior learning assessment program may want to use the performance criteria developed for CAEL by Knapp and Jacobs. The performance criteria should correspond to those already used for regular students, but given the fact that the criteria will be used on adults, the criteria should take into consideration not only intellectual skills, but entrepreneurship skills, interpersonal relations and maturity (Klemp).

There should be a consensus on the connection between the performance criteria and existing courses and training programs in order to help students attain new educational objectives (Heermann; Warren; Withorn and Cedrone; Rydell; Deiro).

In order to obtain an assessment that is fair and equitable and one that respects ethical and moral principles, planners need to ensure that only the learning outcomes demonstrated will be assessed, and never the experience as such, nor the number of years spent on a given task or in a given field. The literature is extremely explicit about this requirement (Fremer; Willingham; Ekstrom and others; Sharon; Avakian and Lipsett; O'Connell; Warren; Martorana and Kuhns; Hrudy; Keeton; Kurtz; Serling; Taaffee and Litwak; Knapp and Jacobs).

RULES FOR GRANTING CREDITS

One question that presents itself in the study of the prior learning assessment literature is whether institutions set limits on the number of credits they grant and if they do, what these limits are. In other words, what is the maximum number of credits an institution will grant for learning acquired outside its walls?

Right at the planning stage, institutions should establish a ceiling on the number of credits they are willing to grant (Ekstrom; Knapp and Jacobs). This ensures that the student will complete his training with a definite amount of new academic learning, which will help to guarantee the validity of the diploma (MacTaggart and Knapp).

The literature mentions a number of possibilities program planners can consider when deciding on the rules for granting credits. For example, some institutions will set a finite limit on the number of credits that can be granted (Keeton; Stanley; Ekstrom; Knapp and Gardiner; MacTaggart and Knapp). Some writers suggest a limit of between 10 and 20 credits (Ekstrom), while others suggest a limit of between 18 and 20, and still others, between 20 and 30 (Fugate and MacTaggart). In some cases, the credits granted can include credits transferred from another institution, acquired through tests, performance examinations or the evaluation of experiential learning (Fugate and MacTaggart). At the planning stage, assessors have the opportunity to reach a general consensus on the maximum number of credits they will grant (MacTaggart and Knapp).

Those involved in the planning of the prior learning assessment program should expect to have to deal with students who request credits for learning that is of an inferior quality; such requests must be rejected (Sackmary and Hedrick).

FINANCING THE PROGRAM

As was mentioned in Chapter 2, one of the reasons why institutions are considering implementing a prior learning assessment program is to improve their financial situation.

According to the literature, the financing of the program is a critical factor (Willingham and Geisinger; Willingham; Keeton; Wolff). A cost analysis has to be made using a different method from the one the institution usually employs (Willingham and Geisinger). Financing prior learning programs has become more complicated in recent years because more credits are being granted and revenues have decreased because of the decline in the younger student population (Knapp).

Because financial resources are limited, program directors have to analyze the various fiscal considerations. MacTaggart and Knapp observe: "In these days of limited resources in higher education, program directors can no longer avoid the fiscal aspects of prior learning programs" (MacTaggart and Knapp 1981, p. 33).

The potential cost of the prior learning assessment program has to be analyzed in relation to the quality of the expected results (Menson). A close study of the expected results will indicate if a prior learning assessment program is a sound investment for the institution.

By reviewing the methods at its disposal to guarantee the quality of its prior learning assessment program, the institution can easily prove the validity of the program to students, parents, employers, patrons and legislators and therefore justify the additional budgetary requirements (Gold; MacTaggart).

BUDGET PARTICULARITIES

When drawing up a budget for a prior learning program, planners will see the differences between the requirements of this program and those of a regular program (Knapp). For one thing, the budget for the first year of operation of the prior learning assessment program differs from that of other types of programs (Sheckley and Warnet). The financing of a prior learning program would be less costly because the program requires less full-time staff, less space and equipment, and fewer support services (MacTaggart). It is also possible to predict that the program will be self-financing, while always remaining accessible to adult students (Heermann and others).

To ensure the sound financing of the prior learning assessment program, a close examination of the situation must be made: for example, the global cost of the program must be evaluated, a list of the necessary resources drawn up, the cost per unit identified, the cost of each resource determined, the number of requests estimated, and a high or low cost defined (Jamison and Wolfe).

It is also important to examine direct expenses (for a specific activity) and indirect expenses (not attributed to a specific activity), reimbursement costs, fixed costs, variable costs, administrative costs and bad debts (MacTaggart).

Program planners must also analyze and evaluate all the costs in relation to all the operations of prior learning assessment so that the fees for students entering the program are as feasible as possible (Willingham). When they conduct their financial evaluation, planners must remember to take into consideration three variables: the prior learning assessment procedure, the students and the institution (Valley).

EXPENDITURES

The principal expenditures incurred will be: the time administrators, counselors and assessors must devote to the program

and the cost of activities, educational material and equipment
(MacTaggart).

Salaries

Counselors and professors should be paid for their participation
in the prior learning assessment program (Knapp and Gardiner).

Other Expenses

Once the salaries of those involved in the project have been
established, professional training and development costs must
be established. These additional costs will include purchasing
required materials, renting a site for the training, consultation
fees, trips, and the cost of using such equipment as computers
and videos (MacTaggart).

REVENUES

Planners can expect that the main source of revenue for the
program will be the tuition paid by the students who wish to
have their prior learning assessed (Willingham and Geisinger;
Jamison and Wolfe; Markovich and Malling).

The literature is quite clear on one point: students must pay for
the number of credits they request, and not for the number of
credits they eventually receive (Sachs). Thus MacTaggart and
Knapp write: "One change that is gaining widespread acceptance among colleges is that students are not and should not be
charged per credit awarded" (MacTaggart and Knapp 1981,
p. 41). Institutions planning to implement a prior learning
assessment program need not worry that students will refuse to
pay the cost of their assessment. An informal survey reports
that a high percentage of students are willing to pay several
hundred dollars to have their skills assessed (Avakian and
Lipsett).

In keeping with ethical and moral principles, planners must
remember that students should be informed in advance that

paying to have their learning evaluated for academic credits does not guarantee in any way that the credits will be granted (Sachs).

Other possible sources of revenue for the project include: contributions made by the institution itself, grants, remuneration from contracts from outside the institution (employers and unions), and educational sabbaticals negotiated with employers or other groups (MacTaggart).

ADVERTISING

Part of the planning process involves informing the community at large of the existence of the prior learning assessment program. Planners can study different possible approaches they might want to try. It seems, however, that word-of-mouth and excellent program materials remain the best publicity (Knapp; Fugate and MacTaggart).

Planners must keep in mind the nature of their student clientele and the educational mission of the institution when planning their promotional campaign. The advertising must be done in a professional manner to reassure the community that the institution's prior learning assessment program will respect the same ethical criteria it applies to its other programs (Heeger).

If institutions wish to make a marketing survey, they have to consider the clientele, the organizational environment, the expertise of the institution, the role of the program in education, an evaluation of the advantages and disadvantages, and the degree of awareness of the population (Heeger).

In conclusion, the planning stage, which precedes the implementation of the prior learning assessment program, is essential. While the planning stage can mean a substantial investment of time, it is well worth it. Careful planning makes the assessment process that much stronger, allowing professionals and adults to experience the process in agreement with the ideological principles developed in Chapter 2.

According to the literature, planners must first consider their reasons for wanting to implement the program. Next, they must predict the characteristics of the program, including how the various operations will be managed and coordinated, the duration of the program, the material resources required, the educational objectives, the expected outcomes, and the student services and human resources required.

Once all of these variables have been examined, the planners can select the staff required for the program. It is important to define the roles of the program administrators, counselors and assessors and prepare professional development programs for them. Admission rules then have to be set, performance criteria defined and rules for granting credits established. Then the question of the financing of the program must be tackled and an advertising campaign planned.

Once all the planning and preparations are complete, it is time for the academic institution and their new clientele to put the prior learning assessment program into operation.

IDENTIFICATION OF THE PRIOR LEARNING

Now that the administrators have taken the time at the planning stage to anticipate various situations as well as alternative solutions to potential problems, the actual process of prior learning assessment can begin. The process starts with the identification of the prior learning outcomes, is followed by the assessment of this learning and concludes with the accreditation of the learning.

CHARACTERISTICS OF THE ADULT STUDENT CLIENTELE

As was shown in Chapter 2, adults acquire new learning in their efforts to fulfill their fundamental and developmental needs in a society that is constantly changing. They see in prior learning assessment a process that allows them to, among other things, obtain an academic degree and bring meaning to their lives.

Nevertheless, many adults do not quite know what to expect when they return to school to have their prior learning assessed because they have been away from the academic world for so long. Indeed, many of the students who enroll in the prior learning assessment program are women who have been away from school for at least 10 to 15 years (Ekstrom).

Many of the adults who enroll in the program are older, mature individuals who have a great deal of life experience and are very attentive to their educational needs (O'Connell). They belong to different age groups and have very different backgrounds (Shipton and Steltenpohl). More and more women are enrolling in prior learning assessment programs (Knapp) and many have not had post-secondary schooling and are not always well-prepared for studying (Magarell).

Many adults lack self-assurance when they return to school; they are not confident that they can meet the challenges that will face them in the educational milieu (Mark and Menson; Thomas and others). Mark and Menson note that "most adults have been out of the academic world for a considerable period of time, and they tend to be both unsure of themselves and unclear about the expectations of the academic environment" (Mark and Menson 1982, p. 65). Some are traumatized by the thought of returning to school (Mahoney); others need to have their basic skills in reading, writing and mathematics verified before they can even consider the possibility of having their prior learning assessed (Rydell).

Using Kolb's findings, Shipton and Steltenpohl affirm that adults return to school with different learning styles, which have developed from their life experience, environment, and hereditary factors. On the subject of learning styles, Shipton and Steltenpohl write: "Some persons, for example, primarily approach problem solving or learning by being active, while others are reflective; some surrender themselves to direct experience, while others apply logic" (Shipton and Steltenpohl 1981, p. 56).

While they often feel their experiences are generally of academic caliber, adults are often fearful of continuing their
learning in an academic institution. As Shipton and Steltenpohl
write, "On the one hand, they tend to see college-level learning
in almost every experiential situation; on the other, they tend to
be apprehensive about their ability to learn in the college setting" (Shipton and Steltenpohl 1981, p. 59).

It is difficult for adults seeking prior learning assessment to
establish the link between their educational objectives and the
identification of their prior learning. Helping adults to clarify
their educational objectives improves their ability to plan their
learning project, a fact which MacTaggart and Knapp confirm
when they write: "Leading students to engage in educational
goal clarification enhances their ability to participate actively in
educational planning and to integrate proper learning into the
total plan" (MacTaggart and Knapp 1981, p. 49).

Writers on prior learning assessment report that the assistance
provided to adults before they have their prior learning assessed
helps them to:

— learn to assess themselves, clarify their objectives and
  develop a career plan;

— learn to assess their academic skills for a specific level of
  study and to develop the necessary skills to do it;

— learn to make the transition between their usual way of
  living to the life of an adult student.

Moreover, adults who return to school to have their prior learning assessed do not always have the same understanding of
what "experiential learning" means. Some believe that the
number of years of experience could replace academic courses,
but, as was mentioned above, the number of years of experience does not necessarily prove that the learning has taken
place. In addition, when an adult is a witness to someone else's
actions, has heard someone discuss a topic or done extensive

reading on a particular subject, this does not necessarily constitute sufficient proof of learning (Keeton and Tate).

Although they naturally want to respond to the requests made by adults, academic institutions cannot automatically grant credits to all those who request them. Schools are responsible for the validity and the reliability of the accreditation they give. They also want their students to be adequately prepared to have their prior learning assessed. The prior learning assessment literature clearly states that even the best prior learning assessment program will not function efficiently if students have not been adequately prepared (Shipton and Steltenpohl; Knapp).

METHODS TO IDENTIFY THE LEARNING

Academic institutions must choose a method to identify prior learning that responds to their expectations as well as those of the students who enroll in the program.

Over the past 30 years, academic institutions have considered the assessment stage at length, studying the various ways to assess prior learning. However, they have not always planned for the identification stage where the prior learning to be assessed is initially specified.

Academic institutions have always used such traditional assessment methods as tests and written exams. When the prior learning students needed to have assessed was in fields such as mathematics, algebra, pure sciences and the like, tests and written exams were efficient methods of evaluation (Ekstrom and others). However, a lot of students were coming to academic institutions with other types of learning that could not be as easily verified and assessed (Mahoney). Standardized tests with multiple-choice questions and written exams were not always giving students the opportunity to express themselves, explain their learning, or give their opinions. As Heermann writes: "To a significant degree, competence in many occupations is interpersonal; existing paper-and-pencil tests inadequately measure the extent of interpersonal effectiveness" (Heermann 1977, p. 27).

Academic institutions therefore had to ask students to explain what they knew through interviews, demonstrations, simulations, and depending on the nature of the learning, through a presentation of their finished products (Ekstrom and others). But in these attempts to identify prior learning, academic institutions found themselves in the difficult position of trying to grapple with the wide variety of learning each student has acquired in order to situate each student with respect to this learning.

Faced with this challenge, institutions came to the conclusion that before they can assess the prior learning, they need to know more about it. To that end, they began to ask adults to create a curriculum vitae. However, the curriculum vitae cannot prove that the learning the person claims to have acquired has actually been acquired.

Interviews can benefit those who have the power of persuasion and are skilled in the art of clearly expressing their point of view; others who do not have these skills are definitely penalized by this assessment method because they are not able to get their message across (Pendergrass and others).

Researchers and others working in the field of prior learning assessment came to the conclusion that taken separately, all of these methods of assessment were not necessarily fair to adults. The methods could neither guarantee that the learning had really been acquired, or that the learning could always be assessed in a valid and reliable way. Adults needed a way to make a complete inventory of all that they had learned so that they could clearly see this knowledge they acquired outside of school for themselves and establish its link with what they will study at school. Mark and Menson write: "Returning adult learners in programs that assess prior learning have usually had experiences in business, community affairs, childrearing, and family life, but they rarely understand fully the developmental tasks that they have mastered, the ways in which they have learned, or the relationship between learning from life experience and learning in the academy" (Mark and Menson 1982, p. 69).

Academic institutions came to the conclusion that not only do adults need to be granted credits, but they need help to develop themselves as human beings (Chickering; Matusak; Knapp and Gardiner). Moreover, since adults are forced to make all kinds of adjustments in their daily lives, they could get discouraged and have trouble persevering with their goals. It was evident, then, that academic institutions had to find a way to help adults learn to persevere (Mahoney).

In essence, then, academic institutions have realized the necessity of finding a method that enables adults to clearly establish their learning so that this learning can be assessed in a way that conforms with established evaluation norms. It was obvious that a method must be designed that helps people position themselves on the academic scale of knowledge (Stack and Hutton). This method would be a necessary prerequisite to assessment, one that adequately prepares students to have their learning assessed. The method that does exactly this is the *portfolio method,* and it is described in detail below.

THE PORTFOLIO METHOD

The portfolio has gained so much importance in the field of prior learning assessment that most writings on the subject make implicit reference to it. Some authors write very explicitly on the subject, most notably Ekstrom and others, Shulman, Withorn and Cedrone, Munce, Dwyer and Torgoff, Fisher-Thompson, Serling, Shipton and Steltenpohl, Heermann and others, Haines and Schwoebel, Krueger, Mark and Menson, Mahoney, and Branch. All agree that the portfolio method has become the method *par excellence,* the preferred method to help adults identify their learning so that this learning may eventually be assessed (Knapp; Forrest; Menson).

It is quite clear in the literature that many institutions have adopted the portfolio method as the best way to assess prior learning (Shulman). With experience, the portfolio has proven to be the surest way to identify prior learning. CAEL's advocacy of the method has helped it to gain such large acceptance, as Knapp confirms when she writes that "as a result of CAEL's advocacy, portfolio assessment has become the chief assessment model in prior learning programs" (Knapp 1981, p. 4).

In the beginning, the portfolio was defined as a written communication an adult creates for the purpose of requesting credits for the learning he has achieved mostly through his life experiences (Stephens College Without Walls). The portfolio was also described as a tabulation of the evidence of prior learning (Pendergrass and others; Knapp and Davis; Shulman).

Since in the portfolio method one of the things adults are required to do is write an autobiography, it was necessary to point out that this is not the only component of the portfolio. Otherwise, it would be too easy for someone with writing skills and a fertile imagination to dream up an unverifiable life story (Stanley).

Today, the portfolio method is defined as the process through which an adult makes an inventory, analysis and synthesis of his learning, classifies it into components that are related to course contents, and collects proof of his learning so that the learning can be assessed by experts (Heermann; Warren and Breen).

With practical experience, it became evident that in keeping with the ideological principles, the portfolio has become a document that gathers all kinds of information about the experiential learning a person has acquired. It has become the best way to identify learning that comes from informal and formal studies, paid and unpaid work, leisure activities and the marker events of a person's life. The portfolio gives adults the opportunity to organize coherently all the learning that might be assessed later. The portfolio is not simply a description of the learning activities the person has engaged in, but a process that permits an analysis of the learning and its supporting evidence (Knapp and Gardiner).

One thing must be clearly understood: the portfolio as such is not assessed. Rather, it is the learning outcomes described in the portfolio that are related to the educational program of the student that are assessed (Knapp and Gardiner).

The majority of adults wishing to have their learning recognized register in a course on portfolio development. They are expected to complete the course on portfolio development, but, needless to say, this is not a guarantee that they will receive the recognition they seek. Rydell writes that "all students who enroll in portfolio development courses are expected to complete the portfolio. However, students are not guaranteed to receive academic credit for their noncollege learning solely on the basis of completing the portfolio" (Rydell 1982, p. x).

Even though developing a portfolio is a long and sometimes difficult process, it becomes in itself an important learning opportunity (Mark and Menson). Indeed, in the process of analyzing all his past accomplishments, an adult might come to know himself better and learn how to reach his short- and long-term life objectives (Mark and Menson). That is why students usually must register in a 45-hour course that is most often a credit course (Fisher-Thompson; Rydell).

No definitive model exists for the portfolio method in the prior learning literature. This may be explained by the fact that a lot of different institutions were experimenting with the method at more or less the same time. Nonetheless, with the help of CAEL's publications, it is possible to see the same logic being used in a number of different institutions (Fugate and MacTaggart).

Usually institutions begin by introducing students to prior learning assessment through a seminar or orientation session (Rydell). During this opening session, adults receive information on the educational system of today and how it operates. It is important to explain that academic institutions have undergone many changes since the adults participating in the session left school. Schools differ from what they were 20 or 30 years ago: many new academic programs exist, new courses are being offered to students and many new options might interest the adults (Schatz and others; Haines and Schwoebel). The orientation session should also include a history of prior learning assessment so that those enrolled in the prior learning assessment program can realize they are not alone in wanting to return to school and seek assessment of their prior learning (Cross).

In order to help adults feel more comfortable in the new academic setting, a person is assigned to assist them through each stage of the portfolio development process (Stevens; O'Connell). Adults receive this help not only because they are adults, but because the changes they are facing are very rapid (Mahoney). Academic institutions assign counselors this task of assisting adults who wish to have their prior learning assessed. In performing this function, the counselor keeps the institution informed about its new adult clientele. Mahoney writes: "Advisors can be a potent force in alerting an institution to the opportunities and issues related to diversity of preparation among students" (Mahoney 1982, p. 78). In many cases, the counselor is also the person who teaches the course on portfolio development (Taaffee and Litwak).

To facilitate the work of all those involved in the prior learning assessment process and the transfer of a student's file from one institution to another, the portfolio development procedure used in many institutions seems to have reached a certain uniformity (Knapp and Gardiner) and consistent structure (Neely and Dees).

Developing a portfolio to identify an adult's prior learning is a prerequisite to the assessment of the learning and the person's return to academic studies. Menson states that "the assessment process is still dominated in most institutions by the practical concerns of preparing a portfolio for faculty evaluation and preparing the student to cope with the university" (Menson 1982*a,* p. 2). Given the very individualized nature of the portfolio method, the person teaching the course on portfolio development must meet each student individually (Gross and others) to verify the content of the portfolio and ensure that the student includes all essential elements when identifying his prior learning (Rydell).

Judging from the procedures currently in use at many institutions, there are two main phases in the process of developing a portfolio. In the first, the student creates an exhaustive, comprehensive portfolio; in the second, he organizes and selects elements from his first portfolio to create a second, final portfolio to submit to assessors.

PHASE ONE: DEVELOPING A COMPREHENSIVE PORTFOLIO

Developing a comprehensive portfolio consists of a series of different operations that enable adults to reflect on, among other things, themselves, their values, their interests and their goals (MacTaggart and Knapp).

Making an Inventory of Life and Work Experiences

Adults begin by reviewing all that they have accomplished in their lives up to the present time. This includes credit and non-credit studies they have pursued, paid and unpaid work they have done, leisure, travel and sports activities they have engaged in, and marker events they have experienced. Making this inventory helps the adult recall different events in his life that may have generated new learning. At this time, the adult should not try to judge the quality of the learning. Knapp and Gardiner state: "First, it is best to encourage the learner to inventory all possible learning experiences without applying criteria or qualifications to the experiences" (Knapp and Gardiner 1981, p. 16).

Making this review of their life and work experiences provides some adults with a unique opportunity to take the time to ponder seriously their life accomplishments so far because, as MacTaggart and Knapp write: "Few adults in our society have the opportunity or time for serious, meaningful self-reflection" (MacTaggart and Knapp 1981, p. 54).

Identifying Life/Career and Educational/Training Objectives

After they have made an inventory of their life and work experiences, adults are ready to begin thinking about their future goals and what their educational objectives need to be so that they can attain these goals. In their report on the educational value of the portfolio, Warren and Breen note the results of studies conducted by Berte, Lehman, and McCoy, which stipulated that by doing this operation of thinking about their future objectives, students learn to organize their thoughts, establish realistic objectives, define their expectations, and plan their own personal development.

This task has bearing on the life accomplishments of adults and their career plans (Rawlings and Davison; Haines and Schwoebel). It gives adults the opportunity to recall goals and objectives they had in the past, but never attained for some reason (lack of money, geographical situation, for example).

This operation also helps adults to better understand the link between their experiential learning and their educational project. As MacTaggart and Knapp write, this is how students learn "to link the assessment of prior learning to educational planning, namely, developing an understanding of the relation between experience and education" (MacTaggart and Knapp 1981, p. 59). The task is important because it is often difficult for homemakers or volunteers, for instance, to make the link between what they have learned and academic learning (Stanley).

Identifying and Verifying Prior Learning and its Correspondence to Credit Courses

Once students have defined their future objectives in relation to an educational program, the next thing they must do is link their prior learning with specific courses in the program in which they wish to register. The idea is to get students to focus on the prior learning they can relate to concrete academic courses. Thus Knapp and Gardiner observe that "the learner needs to determine which of the outcomes are acceptable as college-level learning" (Knapp and Gardiner 1981, p. 16).

At this point in their portfolio preparation, students need to know the criteria used to determine whether experiential learning has educational value. MacTaggart and Knapp write: "What is needed is an understanding of some criteria by which to judge whether an experience has indeed been educative at the college level" (MacTaggart and Knapp 1981, p. 59). These criteria are given later in this book.

A common problem encountered is that adults are not always aware that they have to acquire new learning to attain their educational objectives. Shipton and Steltenpohl state: "Even when adults return to college with clear goals, they have often not acknowledged or understood that new learning will need to take place before they reach their goal" (Shipton and Steltenpohl 1981, p. 55). Therefore, the experience of matching their prior learning with specific academic courses will make it clear to adults that new learning must indeed take place.

Students need to gather documents to support their claims of prior learning. Indeed, any adult wishing to receive academic credit for his prior learning must be prepared to submit proof of his learning (Willingham; Serling; Ekstrom; Rydell). The proof can be written evaluations given by recognized authorities. Knapp and Gardiner write: "What is required by many institutions are evaluative statements by authorities who may be faculty, community experts, former mentors, employers, or co-workers" (Knapp and Gardiner 1981, p. 19). Further, Knapp and Gardiner specify what these supporting documents should contain: "These evaluative statements should attest to the skills and knowledge being evaluated, how well the person can perform, the standards used, and the area of expertise possessed by the evaluator" (Knapp and Gardiner 1981, p. 19). The supporting documents a person provides help to show academic institutions how serious the adult is about his request for prior learning assessment (Rydell).

Planning the Educational Program Plan

Once students have linked their prior learning to specific academic courses, they can make their educational program plan. In the plan, they list all the required courses for the academic program they would like to complete, noting which courses they believe they will not have to take because they have already acquired the learning. This gives students an idea of the number of courses they will need to take to complete the program. If they remain unsure about which educational program they should take, students could enroll in one or two courses to explore the various possibilities offered by the institution (Shipton and Steltenpohl).

On the subject of creating a program plan for education or training, the literature stresses the importance of establishing the link between acquired knowledge and studies to be undertaken, that is, the link between practical and theoretical knowledge in a specific discipline (MacTaggart and Knapp).

The prior learning assessment literature discusses a learning contract that can be made between the student and the institution in which both parties agree on the studies that need to be completed once the assessment of the prior learning has been made (Warren and Breen). The student must enter into this agreement with a clear understanding of the institution's goals, resources and study conditions (MacTaggart and Knapp).

PHASE TWO: ORGANIZING THE PORTFOLIO FOR PRESENTATION TO ASSESSORS

In the process of creating the final version of his portfolio, that is, the portfolio that he will present to assessors, the student gathers together all the relevant documents and supporting materials that have been verified by the counselor/portfolio course instructor (Knapp). The student and counselor meet, usually in tutorial sessions, to review the portfolio to ensure that the student has the maximum chance to obtain the credits he requests (Meyer; Heermann; Stanley; Fisher-Thompson).

Once the student has studied and revised the contents of his portfolio with his counselor's assistance, the student can plan his educational or training program. Once he makes this educational program plan, the student has everything he needs to present his prior learning for assessment to professors or other experts in the field. Because assessors receive a large number of requests from people wanting to have their prior learning assessed, students can facilitate the task of the assessors by providing them with a request that is well-organized.

The prior learning literature does not propose a definitive way to organize the portfolio. This can be explained by the fact that, as was mentioned earlier, prior learning assessment began all across the United States at almost the same time. The literature, particularly the writings of Serling, does nonetheless describe the principal components of the portfolio. The portfolio should begin with a cover page and be followed by a table of contents. Students then describe their principal life experiences, explain their career and training objectives, make a chronological list of their acquired learning that demonstrates the nature and breadth of the learning, create an educational program plan, make an official request for credits and provide supporting documents to prove the knowledge they claim to have. In the end, a portfolio consisting of different types of documents that help to prove the student has acquired academic-level knowledge is submitted to the assessors (Serling).

THE EDUCATIONAL VALUE OF CREATING A PORTFOLIO

According to Warren and Breen, when compared with those who do not, students who experience the entire process of developing their portfolios gain important abilities when it comes to describing their learning and relating this learning to their educational objectives. Krueger adds that adults who take the course on portfolio development improve their self-perceptions and their abilities to learn in certain specific ways.

The increased self-knowledge that comes with developing a portfolio leads to intellectual development and improved communication skills, critical thinking and interrelationships between students, professionals and assessors (Warren and Breen).

In summary, the main objective of the identification stage is to help the adult to make an inventory of everything he knows, analyze the content of his learning, and establish how this learning corresponds to specific courses in his educational or training program. In the process, the adult makes a complete dossier of his learning that institutions can study to determine whether the adult should submit his prior learning for assessment.

ASSESSMENT OF THE PRIOR LEARNING

Once the identification stage has been completed, the student's file is given to the person responsible for organizing the assessment. A copy of the student's file is then sent to every department involved in the assessment process. If, for example, a student requests that his prior learning be assessed for credits in psychology, sociology, and economics, a number of photocopies of the portfolio are sent to each department because there will probably be more than one assessor in each department (Stanley; Fugate and MacTaggart).

Even when a counselor has assisted the student in developing his portfolio, there is no guarantee that credits will be granted (Rydell). The final decision will only be known at the end of the assessment process. This final decision is reached when the assessors decide if the learning outcomes described in the portfolio are in line with the institution's preestablished criteria.

In order to understand the procedure institutions must follow to ensure a valid and reliable assessment, it is necessary to study the prior learning assessment literature on the subject in great detail and isolate the important trends. This careful study of the literature is justified since it is at the assessment stage where the principles of justice and ethics must be most rigorously applied. Fremer comments on the important role the institution must fulfill in providing valid prior learning assessments: "The issue of ethical responsibility . . . should be explicitly identified as a significant one. A commitment to meeting the educational needs of students does not, of course, eliminate the need for colleges to consider the implications for society of decisions made about individual students" (Fremer 1976, p. 19). In essence, institutions have an ethical responsibility towards students and society as well.

Institutions also have an obligation to guarantee that the evaluation procedures used to assess learning can actually verify the abilities the student has acquired. Fremer writes that "an institution's evaluation procedures and standards must be adequate to certify the existence of such competencies" (Fremer 1976, p. 19).

In the early days of prior learning assessment, it was believed that the validity and reliability of an assessment depended only on the extent of the experiential learning. With time and experience, it became evident that the judgment of the assessors and the selection of appropriate evaluation procedures were essential for an appropriate assessment. This fact underlines the importance of a judicious choice of assessors. Thus Knapp and Gardiner remark: "Evaluation concerns focus on three major questions: Who are the assessors? Are their judgments accurate and equitable? What standards are used in prior learning assessments?" (Knapp and Gardiner 1981, p. 22).

CHOOSING ASSESSORS

The people chosen to be assessors are experts in the field of learning to be assessed. On this subject, Reilly writes: "Assessment must, therefore, be placed in the hands of an 'expert,' someone who has specialized knowledge and experience in a relevant discipline or field" (Reilly and others 1977, p. v). Since it is not possible at the planning stage to predict in which specific disciplines the acquired learning will belong, assessors are usually only chosen once a specific request for evaluation has been made.

Normally, assessors are chosen from among the regular professors who teach in the field of learning to be assessed (Kray; Whitaker; Willingham). Heermann writes: "Presumably, these persons are regular faculty members who understand the discipline or occupation in which the student is documenting learning" (Heermann 1977, p. 25). Having regular professors act as assessors of prior learning is one of the strengths of the program. Christensen writes: "The assessment of learning is made by teaching faculty and we believe this is one of the strengths of the program since the same professionals who regularly judge students' performance and award credit in standard programs are exercising their professional competence and responsibility in assessing the learning and competence of students applying for credit equivalency" (Christensen 1975, p. 21). The regular professor brings consistency to the evaluation because he assesses the learning of both student populations: adults and the regular student clientele. The role of the professor in the assessment process is critical and unique (Withorn and Cedrone). His participation is requested in every detail of the assessment process of the program. Ward writes of expert faculty members being involved "not only in every detailed student assessment but in all further refinements in the program" (Ward 1980, p. 63).

The prior learning assessment literature emphasizes the importance of having assessors who are professors or experts in the discipline assessed because of the individual and unique nature of experiential learning (Reilly and others; Erickson; Heermann; Keeton; Shulman; Avakian and Lipsett; Klemp; Kintzer; Martorana and Kuhns; Knapp). Assessors also have the responsibility to decide which learning outcomes are acceptable for credit (Bradley and Bolman). From Willingham's point of view, assessors can expect to fulfill one or several functions:

"They serve several functions which may or may not be performed by the same individual" (Willingham 1977, p. 41).

Sometimes assessors may feel more comfortable working in a team or as part of a jury of assessors because assessing non-traditional learning is not something they do very often. Avakian and Lipsett write: "In some instances, a special evaluation by a panel of experts may be arranged" (Avakian and Lipsett 1979, p. 5).

Assessors may sometimes require the assistance of outside professionals who are known experts in the domain of learning to be assessed. The input of outside experts can be very valuable, as Knapp and Gardiner observe: "Using outside experts usually has a salutary and invigorating effect on the faculty and heightens the community's awareness of the institution" (Knapp and Gardiner 1981, p. 28).

Depending on the nature of the learning to be assessed, assessors can be chosen from among teachers within the same department, a permanent committee composed of professors from different disciplines and departments, outside experts or former students, and sometimes students currently enrolled in the program (Stanley). Outside experts can be found from among those students who have already successfully completed the prior learning assessment process (Whitaker). People who hold responsible positions in the community could be invited (Knapp and Gardiner) as well as people working in the business world (Oxnard). In cases where institutions have to assign experts other than professors for the assessment, these people must have specialized knowledge and real expertise in a specific domain.

SUGGESTED CRITERIA FOR CHOOSING OUTSIDE EXPERTS

There is no ready and easy way for institutions to select appropriate people from the community to act as outside experts.

Indeed, Reilly comments that "there are really no hard and fast rules for identifying experts" (Reilly and others 1977, p. 3).

The institution invites an outside expert to participate in the prior learning assessment process when it is clear that the expert's input can improve the quality of the evaluation. Who qualifies as an expert for evaluating the academic level of an individual's prior learning? Reilly defines who an expert is: "An expert is an individual having special skill or knowledge derived from experience, education or training" (Reilly and others 1977, p. 2). Reilly defines a number of ways to find an outside expert:

1) Recommendations from two or three other experts in the same or a related discipline.
2) Published works (e.g., newspaper or magazine articles, books, etc.) on a given subject.
3) Technical products or artistic works in a related area.
4) A formal academic degree in a related area.
5) Other formal credentials such as a license.
6) Awards or honors for achievement in the field.
7) Teaching experience in the area.
8) Supervisory experience in the same field.
9) Membership in organizations or societies specialized in an area related to the subject.

Reilly suggests that when selecting an outside expert, institutions use more than one of the criteria listed above and make sure that the sources of the information about the expert are good. To facilitate the choice of outside experts, Whitaker writes that the first criteria should be expertise in the field of learning to be assessed as well as expertise in psychometry so that the outside expert will be familiar with the data presented to him and be objective and motivated.

In sum, outside experts must have specific knowledge and abilities and be able to demonstrate their competence with respect to preestablished criteria (Knapp and Gardiner).

Given the fact they will have to judge learning outcomes over which they had no control, assessors must not only be competent in the field of learning, but exhibit good judgment to guarantee the quality of the assessment both for the institution and the adult student. Reilly comments: "It is especially important, then, that the assessors, in addition to being 'experts' in a particular substantive domain, also be competent judges. Experts who are not properly prepared to conduct assessment jeopardize the equity of assessment for the institution, and more importantly, for the individual student" (Reilly and others 1977, p. 1). While the fact that the assessor has good judgment does not always guarantee that the assessment will be perfect, it can assure fair treatment for students, as Reilly writes: "Competent judges, on the other hand, while not guaranteeing perfect assessment, can ensure an equitable and consistent treatment of all students" (Reilly and others 1977, p. 1).

ASSESSMENTS BASED ON THE JUDGMENTS OF ASSESSORS

When experiential learning assessment was in the early stages of its evolution, Warren Willingham, a well-known psychometrist in the field of prior learning assessment, believed that only standardized tests could verify prior learning. However, with experience and further research, Willingham came to a different conclusion. Keeton writes that Willingham "finally came to realize that reliability of assessment is a matter of validity of the inference-making processes in going from the evidence of learning to the conclusion as to what has been learned. . . . It is not a matter of having a standardized instrument" (Keeton 1985, p. 10-11).

Those involved in the assessment of prior learning must consider the methods that can be used to assess different kinds of learning (Pottinger and Goldsmith). In traditional academic institutions, professors usually prepare their own exams (essay-type exams, multiple-choice exams, oral exams) to verify the learning that their students have acquired in the courses they teach. In some cases, notably with the objective multiple-choice exams, there is no possibility to judge if the student has acquired additional skills or skills that are different from those expected. Nor is there any way to determine if other, equally important learning has been acquired. Often the student does not have the possibility to express his ideas and his experience is not always shown through true or false questions. Pottinger and Goldsmith comment on the inadequacies of objective-style evaluations when they write: "We have moved from informal systems of judgment and meaning to formal and mechanical systems; from rich and complex concepts of what is desirable performance to oversimplified and trivial concepts of quality performance; from judgment and valuations of abilities based on observed and felt outcomes to judgments and valuations based on pseudoscientific measures of processes" (Pottinger and Goldsmith 1979, p. vii). Moreover, when assessors attempt to assess prior learning, it can be difficult for them to anticipate the answers expected from adults since they did not take the courses given by the assessors (Ekstrom).

Many authors share Willingham's conclusions with respect to standardized methods of evaluation. It is now generally accepted that the assessment of prior learning is best made through the judgment of faculty members. Thus Strange concludes: "In essence, judgments by college faculty members underlie the methods employed for assessing experiential learning" (Strange 1980, p. 38). Martorana and Kuhns echo this conclusion when they write: "Obviously, awarding credit for experiential learning depends on faculty involvement and judgment" (Martorana and Kuhns 1979b, p. 4). The literature insists that regardless of the way the learning was acquired, the judgment of professors determines the quality and extent of the acquired learning (Reilly and others; Young and Andrews; Serling).

Whatever the assessment procedure employed, the essential element remains the professional judgment made by the teachers in the particular field of knowledge to be evaluated. Spille and others affirm: "A key element in all such methods is professional judgment by faculty in the areas concerned" (Spille and others 1980, p. 7).

A good, appropriate judgment requires objectivity, general and specialized knowledge, as well as honesty and motivation (Central Michigan University). Assessors must consider their judgments and the procedures they use with a critical eye. Knapp and Gardiner write: "Faculty assessors themselves are critical about the quality of their judgments and often evaluate the assessment process itself" (Knapp and Gardiner 1981, p. 28).

CHOOSING ASSESSMENT PROCEDURES

Once the assessors have been recruited and their competence verified and everyone agrees that the evaluation will be based on the judgment of the assessors, a photocopy of the portfolio is given to the assessors so that they can read it and familiarize themselves with its contents (Christensen; Preston). Assessors are expected to select the assessment procedures, structure the assessment process, observe the student during the assessment (for example, during an interview), and judge the relevance of the learning (Reilly and others).

The members of the assessment jury choose the assessment procedures that best suit the nature of the learning identified in the portfolio. Next, they define the assessment criteria based on the assessment procedures they have chosen. These assessment criteria will be used later for reference. Then the assessors judge the quality of the learning, this judgment being essential to a valid and reliable assessment process (Martorana and Kuhns; Serling).

In 1978, Davis and Knapp reported that the assessment procedures most frequently used in two-year public colleges were: performance tests (96%), evaluation of finished products (84%), interviews (80%), portfolios (68%), essays (68%) and simulations (56%). Back then, the portfolio was considered to be just another assessment process, but with experience, it came to be seen as an individual method of evaluation that incorporates all the other evaluation procedures. In a study of the assessment process at seven different institutions, Rydell affirmed that to determine the level of knowledge and abilities, the following procedures were used: finished products, interviews (including oral exams), simulations, case studies and essays done without the supervision of a professor, multiple-choice exams and self-evaluation. Rydell points out that quite often students were invited to discuss with the assessors which assessment procedures they would prefer to submit to.

ASSESSING THE LEARNING OUTCOMES

As was true for the identification of the learning, it is difficult to pinpoint in the literature a definitive procedure for the assessment of the learning. That is probably because throughout the history of prior learning assessment, different techniques have been tried to evaluate the learning. The literature reports on the different techniques that have been used and show the general tendencies that have emerged. For one thing, assessors usually decide on the assessment procedures they will use in advance and determine the expected learning outcomes (Willingham; Cook; O'Connell; Martorana and Kuhns; Ekstrom; Cook and Walbesser; Serling; Silverman and Tate; Stanley; Kurtz; Hrudy; Knapp and Jacobs; Knapp and Gardiner; Loacker; Knapp). The assessment is made based on what a student is able to prove. What the student knows is deemed more important than how he has learned it (Christensen; Ekstrom and others; Nickse; Shulman; Whitaker; O'Connell; Martorana and Kuhns; Stanley; Loacker; Rydell; Deiro). At the time of assessment, the student must be in a position to demonstrate irrevocably the learning he has mastered (Hengesbach; Martorana and Kuhns).

From 1977 onwards, the principles Willingham established in his book *Principles of Good Practice in Assessing Experiential Learning* have been available. These principles can be applied during the identification stage and serve in quite a few institutions as the guidelines for the assessment process (Ranta). Nevertheless, because there is no central authority or organization to control their application, there are variations in the way the principles are applied and interpreted in different academic institutions (Stanley).

Borrowing from Willingham's definitions, to measure learning means to "determine the extent and character of learning acquired"; to evaluate (assess) means to "decide whether the learning meets an acceptable standard and determine its credit equivalency." These two operations remain difficult to separate (Stanley). Indeed, in the early eighties, the two operations of measurement and evaluation have become a single operation, which is referred to as "the assessment." That is why the term "assessment" has been used throughout this book.

Assessors evaluate the experiential learning of a student by judging not only the level, quality and quantity of the learning, but its relevance and relation to the courses in the educational program chosen by the student (Strange).

DEFINING THE ASSESSMENT CRITERIA

The assessment criteria are defined by the assessors to ensure that a just and fair evaluation will be made. According to Knapp and Jacobs, defining the assessment criteria means establishing the criteria to evaluate the experiential learning to determine if it is adequate and deserves credit. Knapp and Jacobs add that the first rule is to grant credits only if the student can demonstrate his learning, and not merely claim that he knows something. Rydell, who studied the evaluation practices of seven institutions for CAEL, said that the most common assessment criteria are as follows:

*Criteria for Identifying the Level of Learning**

1. The **learning must be measurable.** Faculty members focus on knowledge and ability; they have no equitable way of measuring the value of the experience itself.

---

* Adapted from Susan T. Rydell, *Creditable Portfolios: Dimensions in Diversity. A CAEL Resource Manual.* (Columbia, Maryland: Council for Adult and Experiential Learning, 1982).

2. The **learning must have both a theoretical and an applied component.** Many adults are strong in applied knowledge, but may lack a firm theoretical base.

3. The **learning must be academic level.** Typically, a person may receive credit only for learning that is of comparable level to what academic institutions teach in their classrooms.

4. The **learning must be applicable outside the specific context in which it was learned and must serve as a base for further learning.** The person must be able to apply the knowledge and skills in more than one setting.

5. The **learning must be relatively current.** The person may not expect to receive academic credit for knowledge and skills that were acquired some time ago and have been forgotten.

6. The **learning must show some relationship to the person's degree goal.**

In recent years, Whitaker has further refined this criteria to reflect the new knowledge and developments in the field of prior learning assessment. Whitaker writes that in order to be credited for a particular program of study, the adult's learning must:*

— not have previously been recognized (that is, used to fulfill the requirements for a diploma or degree that has been successfully obtained);

— strike a balance between theoretical knowledge and practical application appropriate to the subject;

— correspond to a given academic level;

— be appropriate to the academic context in which credit is requested;

---

* Adapted from Urban Whitaker, *Assessing Learning — Standards, Principles, & Procedures* (Philadelphia: Council for Adult and Experiential Learning, 1989), p. xvii.

— be verifiable by assessors in terms of *what the adult knows* and/or *what the adult can do* and/or *what the adult is.*

Only the learning outcomes are assessed in relation to specific courses (Willingham; Withorn and Cedrone; Loacker; Knapp and Gardiner; Rydell). These learning outcomes can be knowledge, skills, attitudes and behavior acquired or developed outside the traditional academic environment.

The word "competence" is often used in the prior learning assessment literature and it can create a lot of confusion. Whitaker said that once the concept of competence is introduced, it must be defined in terms of standards. To define competence in terms of standards means to determine for a specific competence all the knowledge and skills required, the underlying values and all the "savoir-être" that grants a person the status of being competent (Wolfe). It is easy to understand, then, the difficulty to grasp the meaning behind the word "competence" and even more so, the difficulty to make an exact measurement of competence. Martorana, Kuhns and other authors recommend that taxonomies of competence be developed to help measure various elements of competence, it not being possible to measure competence in its entirety. Until such taxonomies are available, authors like Bradley and Bolman, Mahoney and Chickering suggest using Bloom's taxonomies on the psychomotor, cognitive and affective domains. Klemp states that once competence is defined at the conceptual level, assessment should easily demonstrate the means by which the competence was defined.

Regardless of the criteria used for assessment, the authors of the prior learning assessment literature seem to agree that the standards of quality should be at least as high as those established for regular courses, and these standards should be maintained to ensure the credibility of the institution and the assessment program.

DETERMINING THE NUMBER OF CREDITS

Once assessors have rendered their judgment on the learning outcomes, they must decide on the number of credits they will grant to the student. While the maximum number of credits an institution will grant varies from institution to institution, there is no record in the literature of an institution issuing a full degree. This is because every student is expected to follow a minimum number of courses to complement his non-traditional learning.

As was discussed in Chapter 2, a limit to the number of credits to be granted is usually established by the institution during the planning stages of the prior learning assessment program. Institutions feel that school is still the first place to acquire learning, especially when it comes to studies leading to master's or doctoral degrees. Moreover, some authors are convinced that granting too large a number of credits can create serious problems with the level of graduates' competencies. Knapp voices this concern when she writes that "the granting of credit for prior learning, especially if the number of credits is considerable, could lead to the production of unprepared scholars with diminished competence" (Knapp 1982, p. 49).

To summarize: the assessment stage follows the identification stage. Once a student has identified his learning, completed his portfolio and had the content of the portfolio verified by a counselor, the portfolio is submitted for assessment. The first main operation in the assessment stage consists of choosing assessors according to the knowledge they have in the field of learning to be assessed. Then the assessment proceeds based upon the judgment of the professors, teachers, or, depending on the nature of the learning, outside experts selected to be the assessors. The assessors then discuss and agree upon the best evaluation procedures to use to assess the learning reported in the portfolio. Depending on the nature of the learning, the student may have provided documents to prove what he knows and can do. The student may also have to demonstrate his knowledge through exams, tests, interviews, simulations or finished products. The learning outcomes are evaluated using established criteria, which have already been defined by CAEL and Whitaker. Once the learning outcomes have been assessed, assessors agree on the number of credits to be granted.

Once the assessment has been made, the student's file is reviewed by the assessors. Heermann suggests that more than one evaluator should review the student's file (Heermann). The director of the prior learning assessment program then verifies that all the criteria have been met (Christensen). An appeals process should be made available to students who feel that the results of the assessment are not satisfactory or that they have been cheated (Central Michigan University). A different assessment committee must then be formed (Heermann). In the case where a student has provided false documents, those responsible for the prior learning assessment program have the right to render the results of the assessment null and void (Central Michigan University).

ACCREDITATION

Once the assessors have judged the student's learning outcomes, they send the student's complete file along with their credit recommendation to the official responsible for granting credits at the institution (Fugate and MacTaggart). Official accreditation is the last step in the prior learning assessment process. In this final step, the acquired knowledge is given official recognition, either in the form of a special mention, grade or some other type of notation that guarantees that the student does indeed possess the abilities evaluated.

This final step is very important for the student. In this step, the student's prior learning, which he acquired mostly outside of a traditional academic setting, is recognized. This official recognition gives the student the passport that permits him to engage in further studies. Accreditation is also an official appreciation and recognition of the effort the student has made to acquire knowledge (Sweet). Official accreditation enables the student to clearly see what learning or knowledge he lacks. This incites him to complete his knowledge by pursuing further studies to obtain an academic degree.

There are four main points in the discussion of accreditation in the prior learning assessment literature. They are: the actual practice of accreditation in academic institutions, transcripts, the acceptance of credits by other institutions, and a review of the entire process.

ACCREDITATION IN PRACTICE

In the prior learning assessment literature, there is no definitive model for issuing credits for a student's prior knowledge (Stanley). The discussion about issuing credits for prior learning continues within institutions: opinions are mixed and different reasons are expressed. As a result, no consensus has been reached as yet. The problem is compounded by the fact that the recognition of the learning acquired prior to admission within an institution is not always understood and accepted by professors, especially in higher education (Knapp 1979, p. 15).

In 1977, Willingham observed that traditional courses are not always an accurate way to describe experiential learning. Moreover, experiential learning does not always correspond to the courses included within the institution's academic programs calendar (Rawe 1979, p. 24).

TRANSCRIPTS

Once the assessment process has been completed, a transcript is issued. Rawe writes: "The transcript credential is the only means third parties have for knowing about the learning and how it contributes to a degree" (Rawe 1979, p. 24). Willingham and Warren agree. They believe that a transcript is the only way to make third parties aware of the kind of learning that has been assessed and the value that has been given to it. Because it indicates the credits granted and the level of equivalency, the transcript is the most accepted means to provide information on a student's performance. Erickson writes: "The transcript of course credits and grades is the accepted currency for the exchange of information about levels of performance achieved by students" (Erickson 1977, p. 5). An academic transcript is as necessary to employers as it is to other academic institutions (Nickse). Indeed, just about every author writing about transcripts confirmed their importance. Transcripts have a great deal of importance in the prior learning assessment process because they serve to officially acknowledge the results of the assessments made (Knapp and Gardiner 1981, p. 29).

REPORTING THE CREDITS ON THE ACADEMIC TRANSCRIPT

The methods for reporting the credits granted through prior learning assessment on the transcript vary greatly. Nevertheless, regardless of the methods used, Stanley confirms that the transcript must provide a reliable and complete report of all the learning the student has acquired (Stanley). Stanley observes that many institutions write an equivalent course or subject title instead of the title of an existing course. She adds that it is useful to include a description of the circumstances under which the learning has been acquired, but cautions that this description could be difficult to interpret and compare with traditional transcripts. In order for the process to be more accurate and complete, institutions have chosen a description that specifies the nature of the learning acquired, the assessment techniques used and the identity and qualifications of the assessors involved (Stanley).

Writers on prior learning assessment often wonder what the ideal way to describe the credits given on an academic transcript could be. Different questions are raised and many suggestions are put forward. Some institutions do not give a grade for acquired learning and distinguish this type of learning from supervised learning in a classroom (Knapp 1979, p. 18). The results of many surveys indicate that providing a grade for experiential learning on the transcript complicates matters. After studying the many different methods used by institutions, Knapp recommends including along with the transcript a written explanation why no grade is given for certain courses. The student must be informed right from the beginning that the absence of some grades on his transcript may sometimes penalize him, making it more difficult for him to be admitted to an institution of higher education (Knapp). Therefore, Knapp recommends including more information along with the transcript (a curriculum vitae for personal use, one for employers, and one for institutions of higher education). In the Empire State College Degree Program, instead of the usual transcript, a description of all the work the student has completed is created and used as a transcript (Serling 1980, p. 50).

The important thing to remember is to provide enough information so that teachers who conduct the admission interview will understand the student's background and all the learning he has acquired to date (Knapp).

A student who has received credits for his prior learning definitely wants these credits to have as much value as traditional credits (Sweet). For whatever the reason, whether it be a job change or a move to another location, the student may find himself wanting another institution to be able to interpret the transcript. Warren suggests that the transfer of credits to another institution will be facilitated if the following information is given: first, the intellectual content of the credited experience; second, the general nature of the activities; and third, the level of competence acquired and demonstrated by the student (Warren 1979, p. 98). For example, at Webster College in St. Louis, the credits obtained for experiential learning are clearly differentiated in the transcript from regular credits by the mention that these credits were recognized through an exam. After that, the name of each assessor is given as well as the course title (Fugate and MacTaggart 1983, p. 31).

CRITERIA FOR TRANSCRIPTS

Willingham, who devoted years of research to find a systematic process to recognize prior learning, recommended in 1977 that criteria be established for reporting credits on the academic transcript and made some suggestions. These are some of Willingham's suggestions: the learning should be indicated in an appropriate manner, the credits should be clearly indicated, a description and explanation of the results should be given when the learning is very individualized, and descriptive information should be included when the learning is related to specific courses.

Next, Willingham said that a description of the content and the level of the learning should also be given. This description must indicate the circumstances in which the learning has been acquired and additional information to specify the nature of the learning in such a way that third parties (admission officers or employers) could very easily understand the nature of the learning.

Last of all, Willingham recommends that the following measures be taken: directives regarding the content of the transcript should be established, and when necessary, procedures to obtain and review the assessment results should be developed. In addition, students should be informed in advance of how the information is usually given on the transcript, and the right to confidentiality should be guaranteed for all those directly or indirectly responsible for the information given in the official transcript.

The transcript and the way in which the credits are indicated on it are so important that documents exist to ensure that rigorous rules are applied in the creation of official transcripts. Using the CAEL checklist and the *Academic Record and Transcript Guide,* published by the American Association of Collegiate Registrars and Admissions Officers (AACRAO), Rawe suggests that institutions:

— include all the information that a third party would want to find in a transcript in order to have the best understanding of the assessment of the prior learning;

— indicate the circumstances under which the learning took place: traditional courses, extension courses, correspondence courses, credits obtained by exams, military service;

— use a reference scale, key or legend to describe the standards used (preferably in an attached document).

Other recommendations are given below to help further clarify the information presented in the transcript (Rawe). Institutions should:

— create and use a guide to ensure that all essential elements are included;

— describe the prior learning assessment process with respect to the goals and objectives of the institution;

— explain accurately to third parties the methods used to assess prior learning (in a text on the transcript or in an attached legend);

— explain the prior learning assessment process and the way in which information is indicated on the transcript.

Given the fact that the transcript is the means by which the student can have his experiential learning validated, it is important that the credits granted in each domain be indicated (Sachs).

Because prior learning assessment is a relatively new procedure, Sweet recommends that academic institutions who credit experiential learning avoid using a different vocabulary for prior learning, and assign as much value and importance to this type of learning as they do to traditional learning.

Because accreditation is the way to communicate information to the public, Knapp and Gardiner recommend that institutions:

— describe the prior learning assessment process and link it to the objectives of the institution;

— explain accurately to third parties the methods and standards used to recognize prior learning and inform students about the type of information provided in the transcripts;

— use several types of annotations or transcripts;

— present the content of the transcripts in a way that facilitates the return of students to studies in other institutions (as well as their own).

ACCEPTING CREDITS GRANTED BY OTHER INSTITUTIONS

When a student has had his prior learning officially recognized, he naturally wants other institutions to recognize the credits he has obtained for his prior learning. Because prior learning assessment is still a fairly recent process, academic institutions who have not yet implemented such a program are often hesitant about accepting the credits recognized by another institution. Such institutions tend to limit the number of credits they will accept for the educational program of the new student (Ekstrom and Eliason; Kintzer).

REVIEWING THE ACCREDITATION PROCESS

In summary, the prior learning assessment literature does not present a definitive model for the accreditation stage, but the importance and necessity of the transcript are emphasized. Because it includes a description of all the credits obtained, the transcript allows students to make others aware of what they know. The transcript must be made according to specific criteria, which should give it credibility.

Having an institution recognize credits granted by another institution is not always easy; institutions often limit the number of credits they are willing to accept from elsewhere.

In order to improve the practice of the prior learning assessment process, Reilly suggests a regular evaluation of the entire process. According to Reilly, this periodic evaluation involves verifying the integrity of the assessment procedures, the reliability of the judges, the way the process is carried out, and the performance of the students as well as the possibility of errors.

METHODOLOGICAL PRINCIPLES OF PRIOR LEARNING ASSESSMENT

One point stressed in the literature is the necessity to ensure that prior learning assessment is founded on the ideological principles described in Chapter 2. In order to have the principles of justice and equity, ethics and morals and responsibility respected, four stages of the prior learning assessment process have been developed.

In the first, the **planning stage,** all the important operations of the process are planned. The planning is essential and must be completed before the institution can proceed any further with the assessment of prior learning. Once the planning is complete, institutions can undertake the second stage, the **identification of the learning outcomes** by the students. This is done more and more often through the development of a portfolio. A counselor guides the student through this stage. The third stage, the **assessment stage,** allows the specialists in a specific learning content to assess the learning that was reported in the portfolio. Outside experts may be called in to assist with the assessment. The fourth stage is the **accreditation stage.** In this final stage, a student receives official recognition for his prior learning. The information is recorded on a transcript.

Through a rigorous examination of the way institutions are recognizing prior learning, it is possible to identify the methodological principles that evolve from the ideological principles. These methodological principles reflect the desire to respect justice and equity, ethics and morals and responsibility. The methodological principles are the following: *inventory, analysis, synthesis* and *assessment.*

The principles are defined below, using the definitions given in the Robert and Webster dictionaries as they can be applied to prior learning assessment.

An *inventory* is a review and careful study of all the elements involved in the prior learning assessment process.

An *analysis* is a detailed study of something to discern its important elements, as when the entire process of prior learning is studied to find its essential elements.

A *synthesis* is a series of mental operations that allow the individual to proceed from separate elements or concepts to a coherent whole. A synthesis involves organizing the separate operations in the recognition of prior learning into a comprehensive process that is relatively easy to follow.

An *assessment* involves making an appraisal or value judgment about every operation of every step in the prior learning assessment process so that the methods used to assess prior learning adequately meet the ideological principles.

These four methodological principles are found repeatedly in the prior learning assessment process, as is explained below.

DURING THE PLANNING STAGE

When administrators decide to implement a prior learning assessment program, they must examine their reasons or motives for offering the program. Then they study each principal characteristic of the program and develop a policy on prior learning assessment that deals with the management, coordination, scope and duration of the program. This policy has to satisfy the institution's needs as well as those of the students. Later, administrators think about the resource materials they require and study the possibility of using the resources currently available to them. They review the educational objectives of both the returning students and the educational institution. Administrators also try to predict the impact the program will have. The program may mean, for example, a growth in their adult clientele and the institution's revenue.

DURING THE IDENTIFICATION STAGE

In the second, identification stage of the prior learning assessment process, specific methods are used to identify the often diverse prior learning students have acquired. The portfolio appears to be the most helpful and fair method for identifying prior learning. The portfolio method consists of two distinct phases: the development of the comprehensive portfolio and then the organization of the portfolio for presentation to assessors. When they prepare their comprehensive portfolios, students make a complete review of their life and work experiences, identify their career and learning objectives, identify and verify their prior learning and its correspondence to credit courses, and plan their educational program. Having a student identify his prior learning enables him to review what he has learned so far and distinguish between what can be linked to his educational program and what cannot. The student will be able to assemble similar learning components in relation to specific courses. He himself will make a preliminary evaluation of which learning is of academic value, and gradually build his case for presentation to assessors. The counselor carefully reviews what the student has reported in his portfolio and verifies that the student understands what particular learning is related to his educational program plan. Then, although the responsibility of the counselor is not to judge the quality of the learning outcomes, he can nonetheless estimate the student's chances of receiving credits. In the second phase in which students organize their portfolios for presentation to assessors, students organize all the essential and relevant elements of their comprehensive portfolios into a clear dossier.

DURING THE ASSESSMENT STAGE

In the assessment stage, assessors are chosen for their expertise in the content of the learning reported in the portfolio. Assessors are usually professors specialized in a specific discipline, and when necessary, they can be experts from outside the institution. Outside experts are chosen using very specific selection criteria. They must not only possess the specific knowledge required for the assessment, but they must also exhibit sound judgment. The impartial, appropriate judgment of the assessors is the cornerstone of the assessment process. The content of the portfolio is carefully reviewed and analyzed, and the most accurate assessment procedures are chosen. The learning is assessed, based on preestablished criteria, and assessors verify that the learning has indeed been acquired. They then compare learning outcomes to selected courses and judge the value of the learning. Finally, the number of credits to be granted is determined by the assessors.

DURING THE ACCREDITATION STAGE

During this final stage, the official at the institution responsible for accreditation reviews all the documents one final time and studies the results of the assessment that must be reported on the transcript. The results are reported on the transcript using previously established criteria that must be strictly adhered to not only for the good of the granting institution, but for the good of other institutions who might later receive the student.

To ensure that the ideological principles have been respected during the entire process, academic institutions take advantage of this last stage to review the entire process.

The four methodological principles—*inventory*, *analysis*, *synthesis* and *assessment*—are an integral part of the entire process to recognize prior learning. They enable the prior learning assessment process to reach its ultimate goal: the accreditation of prior learning. These four methodological principles support the ideological principles identified in Chapter 2, and complete this study of the principles of prior learning assessment.

CONCLUSION

This research was undertaken to identify the principles underlying prior learning assessment that are evident in the American literature on the subject. The research was limited to post-1945 publications, concentrating mainly on those published between the years 1974 and 1986, the years when prior learning assessment really soared in the United States.

The main sources consulted were the ERIC Clearinghouse Data Bank for Adult, Career and Vocational Education, the publications of the Cooperative for the Assessment of Experiential Learning (CAEL), and the *New Directions for Experiential Learning* series published by Jossey-Bass Incorporated.

After making an inventory of and selecting the documents, it became apparent that the expression "experiential learning" was used to refer to supervised learning (in the classroom, for instance, or during traineeships and internships) as well as the non-supervised learning that a person acquires throughout his lifetime and outside the academic setting for the most part. Since the objective of this research was to explore this second type of learning, which is often called prior learning, only the documents dealing with this type of learning were retained for further study.

Next, the different meanings of the word "principles" were analyzed. There are three key definitions of the word: the first is "fundamental, origin, source or starting point"; the second, "rule or law"; and the third, "motives or reasons." This last meaning was retained for the purposes of this research.

One of the difficulties encountered in this study was that no document identifies the principles of prior learning assessment as such. In consequence, a very careful and thorough study of all the documents had to be made to isolate and organize the themes emerging in the literature and to classify the different tendencies leading to the principles. Two categories of principles were identified: ideological and methodological. The ideological principles deal with the reasons or motives why adults and institutions wish to get involved in prior learning assessment; the methodological principles deal with the methods and procedures used to recognize prior learning that respect the ideological principles.

This research revealed that the phenomenon of change and the needs of adults to maintain and develop motivate them to want to have their prior learning recognized. Adults want to get a degree and give meaning to their lives. Academic institutions also have their reasons to recognize prior learning. Confronted as they are with numerous and simultaneous social changes, institutions are faced with heavy competition in the business of providing education. Institutions hold the responsibility to ensure that degrees awarded are subjected to impartial and comprehensive rules. Prior learning assessment represents, for academic institutions, a solution to a number of their financial problems: while grants have been reduced, expenses keep increasing and schools are fully aware of the potential income that the new adult clientele represents.

Professors have been forced to face the phenomenon of change, not only as adults but as professionals working in academic institutions that are themselves undergoing changes. For example, faced with a reduction in grants and the arrival of a clientele from diverse backgrounds, the functions performed by professors are more than ever limited to teaching and research. They do not always find in their environment the intellectual stimulation they need to face up to new challenges brought about and imposed on them by change. Prior learning assessment would provide them with a new and interesting challenge: the challenge of assessing and recognizing learning acquired without their supervision.

Academic institutions are pressured by many adults to look at their particular situation. Institutions want to devise methods that will be fair to all, but they also want to give themselves enough time to review the entire situation point by point and then decide on the actions to be taken. Because of their broad social mission, academic institutions have a tremendous responsibility with respect to the methods they will choose to assess adults' prior learning.

Consequently, the ideological principles brought to the forefront in this study are those of *justice* and *equity*, *ethics* and *morals* and, finally, *responsibility*. These ideological principles support the prior learning assessment process as well as the methods used to bring about this process. The authors seem to agree that the method most suitable to honor these principles and satisfy the needs of both adults and institutions is the portfolio method.

The process to recognize prior learning consists of four stages: planning, identification, assessment and accreditation. Each stage is organized according to rules intended to guarantee that the ideological principles are respected. These rules, which are called methodological principles, are: *inventory, analysis, synthesis* and *assessment.*

In this study, the expressions "some principles," and "the principles" are intentionally employed because it is very likely that not everything has been said on the subject. Other researchers with other methods might make different conclusions without contradicting those made here.

Prior learning assessment is an expanding field and all those professionals involved in adult education will want to read and understand the principles defined in this study before beginning to implement a prior learning program in their own institution. The interest other researchers or practitioners will have in this research comes from the attempt this study makes to identify the ideological and methodological principles that are implicit and scattered throughout a large number of publications.

Employers as well as volunteer associations could benefit from the results of this research because they will better understand the needs of adults who have to cope with the phenomenon of change and the reasons that motivate them to seek prior learning assessment. Employers and volunteer organizations could also use the ideological and methodological principles to identify, assess and accredit the learning of those among their staff or volunteers who have acquired on-the-job experience. This assessment and accreditation will lead the staff/volunteers to seek training in fields where they have less knowledge and ability. This research could also help professional associations and unions to establish new criteria for their members that takes an individual's practical experience into consideration.

The results of this research could be used as a starting point for further research. Some suggestions are given here. Further on the subject of resistance to change and the possibilities of adapting to change, a study could be made to analyze how different adults use their time and how well they satisfy their maintenance and developmental needs. Adults who return to school still have to earn a living, care for their families, do volunteer work and set aside time for leisure activities. As far as academic institutions are concerned, it would be interesting to study the possibility of new alliances between schools and other providers of education to guarantee the validity and reliability of the accreditation process. Researchers who are interested in the financial situation of academic institutions could make forecasts concerning the potential new markets that prior learning assessment would bring. It would be interesting as well to study the new possibilities that prior learning assessment offers to professors whose previous experience consisted in teaching and evaluating learning acquired in a traditional manner under their own supervision.

It is to be hoped, then, that this study of the principles will prove helpful to those currently involved in prior learning assessment, whether they be students, administrators, counselors and professors, and at the same time be an impetus for further research in this burgeoning field of prior learning assessment.

BIBLIOGRAPHY

Prior Learning Assessment

Allen, Richard J., and Frederic Jacobs. "Concluding Comments." In *Expanding the Missions of Graduate and Professional Education. New Directions for Experiential Learning,* Vol. 15. San Francisco: Jossey-Bass Inc., 1982.

Avakian, Nancy A., and Laurence Lipsett. "Assessment of Noncollege Learning. AIR Forum 1979 Paper." Paper presented at the Nineteenth Annual Forum of the Association for Institutional Research, May 13-17, 1979. San Diego.

Axelrod, Joseph. "Cross-Cultural Learning: The Language Connection." In *Cross-Cultural Learning. New Directions for Experiential Learning,* Vol. 11. San Francisco: Jossey-Bass Inc., 1981.

Beier, Juliet J., and Ruth B. Ekstrom. "Creating Employment Equity through the Recognition of Experiential Learning." *Journal of Career Education,* 6, 1 (September 1979): 2-11.

Berte, N.R. "Individualization and Contracting." In *New Directions for Higher Education,* 10. Edited by N.R. Berte. San Francisco: Jossey-Bass Inc., 1975.

Bradley, Paul A., Jr., and Susan Olson Bolman. "Faculty Role in Clarifying Student Learning Outcomes." In *Clarifying Learning Outcomes in the Liberal Arts. New Directions for Experiential Learning,* Vol. 12. San Francisco: Jossey-Bass Inc., 1981.

Branch, Audrey, et al. *Learning from Experience. A Handbook for Adult Women Students.* Long Island City: La Guardia Community College, 1982.

Breen, Paul, et al. *Learning and Assessing Interpersonal Competence—A CAEL Student Guide.* Columbia, Maryland: Cooperative Assessment of Experiential Learning, 1977a.

Breen, Paul, et al. *Teaching and Assessing Interpersonal Competence—A CAEL Student Guide.* Columbia, Maryland: Cooperative Assessment of Experiential Learning, 1977b.

Burley, Jo-Ann E. *Andragogy: Implication for Pre-Service/In-Service.* (Vol. 1) American Association of Community and Junior Colleges, 1985.

Bushnell, David S. "Articulating Vocational Education at the Postsecondary Level." In *Transferring Experiential Credit. New Directions for Experiential Learning,* Vol. 4. San Francisco: Jossey-Bass Inc., 1979.

Cantin, Gabrielle. "Fondements de la reconnaissance des acquis de forma-
    tion: Des Questions Préalables." ("The foundations of the recognition
    of prior learning: preliminary questions.") Paper from the Conference
    on the Recognition of Prior Learning, Sherbrooke, May 23-25, 1984.
    Sherbrooke: Université de Sherbrooke, 1984.

Cantin, Gabrielle, et al. "Rapport du Comité d'évaluation de l'expérience du
    Cégep de St-Félicien concernant la reconnaissance des acquis en tech-
    niques infirmières." ("Report of the evaluation committee of the
    St-Félicien College experience of recognizing prior learning in the
    nursing program.") In *Études et Réflexions. Fédération des Cégeps du
    Québec,* Doc. 4. Montreal: 1985.

Central Michigan University. *The Evaluation of Experiential Learning:
    Guidelines for Evaluation Concerning Graduate Student Evaluation.*
    Mount Pleasant, Michigan: Institution for Personal and Career Devel-
    opment, November 1977.

Chickering, Arthur W. *Experience and Learning: An Introduction to Experi-
    ential Learning.* New Rochelle, New York: Change Magazine Press,
    1977.

————. "Education, Work, and Human Development." In *Making Spon-
    sored Experiential Learning Standard Practice. New Directions for
    Experiential Learning,* Vol. 20. San Francisco: Jossey-Bass Inc.,
    1983.

Christensen, Frank A. "Guidelines and Procedures for the Assessment of
    Experiential Learning and the Election and Training of Field Experts."
    In *CAEL Institutional Report No. 5. Cooperative Assessment of Expe-
    riential Learning Project.* Princeton: William Rainey Harper College,
    September 1975.

Christopulos, Diana, and Dudley H. Hafner. "A Model Partnership: The
    American Heart Association and Higher Education." In *New Partner-
    ships: Higher Education and the Nonprofit Sector. New Directions for
    Experiential Learning,* Vol. 18. San Francisco: Jossey-Bass Inc.,
    1982.

Community Colleges of Vermont. *Student Progress Portfolio.* Montpelier,
    1978.

Cook, Marvin T. *Developing Program Maps.* Module 1 of the *Handbook on
    Clarifying College Learning Outcomes.* Columbia, Maryland: Council
    for the Advancement of Experiential Learning, 1978.

Cook, Marvin T., and H.H. Walbesser. *Developing Assessment Tasks.* Mod-
    ule 3 of the *Handbook on Clarifying College Learning Outcomes.*
    Columbia, Maryland: Council for the Advancement of Experiential
    Learning, 1980.

Craig, Robert L., and Christine J. Evers. "Employers as Educators: The 'Shadow Education System.'" In *Business and Higher Education: Toward New Alliances. New Directions for Experiential Learning,* Vol. 13. San Francisco: Jossey-Bass Inc., 1981.

Cross, Patricia K. "Perspectives on Lifelong Learning." Speech given before the Northern California Adult Education Association Interest Group, San Francisco, September 13, 1978.

————. *Adults as Learners.* San Francisco: Jossey-Bass Publishers, 1981.

Davis, L.L., and Joan Knapp. *The Practice of Experiential Education.* Columbia, Maryland: Council for the Advancement of Experiential Learning, 1978.

Deiro, Judy. *Prior Learning Experiences: Handbook for Portfolio Process. Alternative Learning Experiences.* Bellingham, Washington: Whatcom Community College, 1983.

De Meester, Lynn A. "Incentives for Learning and Innovation." In *Business and Higher Education: Toward New Alliances. New Directions for Experiential Learning,* Vol. 13. San Francisco: Jossey-Bass Inc., 1981.

Doherty, Austin, et al. "Toward a Theory of Undergraduate Experiential Learning." In *Learning by Experience—What, Why, How. New Directions for Experiential Learning,* Vol. 1. San Francisco: Jossey-Bass Inc., 1978.

Dwyer, Richard, and Carl Torgoff. "A Labor College." In *Building New Alliances: Labor Unions and Higher Education. New Directions for Experiential Learning,* Vol. 10. San Francisco: Jossey-Bass Inc., 1980.

Ekstrom, Ruth B. "Assessing Re-entry: Women's Life Experience Learning." Paper presented at the Annual Conference of the American Personnel and Guidance Association, St. Louis, Missouri, April, 1981.

————. *Project HAVE Skills—A Program for Matching Women and Jobs.* Princeton: Educational Testing Service, 1981.

————. *Making Experience Count in Sex Equity Programs: A Guide to Help State Sex Equity Coordinators Work with Employers and Adult Women to Further the Recognition of Women's Job-Relevant Life Experience Learning.* Princeton: Educational Testing Service, 1981.

Ekstrom, Ruth B., and Carol N. Eliason. *The Transferability of Women's Life Experience Competencies to Employment and Vocational Education: A State-of-the-Art Review.* Princeton: Educational Testing Service, 1979.

Ekstrom, Ruth B., and M. Lockheed. *Evaluation of the Academically Creditable Competencies Acquired by Women from Domestic and*

Volunteer Work. Final Report. Princeton: Educational Testing Service, 1976.

Ekstrom, Ruth B., et al. *Counseling Implications of Re-entry Women's Life Experiences.* Project Report, Task A4, Project ACCESS. Princeton: Educational Testing Service, 1980.

Ekstrom, Ruth B., et al. *How to Get College Credit for What You Have Learned as a Homemaker and Volunteer.* Princeton: Educational Testing Service, 1981.

Ekstrom, Ruth B., et al. *Making Experience Count in Vocational Education: A Guide to Help Vocational Educators Identify and Provide Recognition to Adult Women Who Have Vocationally-Relevant Life Experience Learning.* Princeton: Educational Testing Service, 1981.

Eliason, Carol. *Equity Counseling for Community College Women.* Washington: Center for Women's Opportunities, American Association of Community and Junior Colleges, 1979a.

————. "The Importance of Research on Transferable Skills to Female Mid-Life Career Changers." Paper presented at the Conference of the National Center for Research in Vocational Education, Columbus, Ohio, June 15, 1979b.

Erickson, Stanford C. "Teachers and New Arrangements for Learning." In *Criteria for the Evaluation, Support, and Recognition of College Teachers,* No. 5. Ann Arbor: Center for Research on Learning and Teaching, Michigan University, 1977.

Evans, Marlene J., et al. "Rethinking and Implementing Outcome Clarification." In *Clarifying Learning Outcomes in the Liberal Arts. New Directions for Experiential Learning,* Vol. 12. San Francisco: Jossey-Bass Inc., 1981.

Fisher-Thompson, Jeanne. "Obtaining a Degree: Alternative Options for Re-Entry Women." Field Evaluation Draft. Association of American Colleges, Project on the Status and Education of Women, Washington, 1980.

Forrest, Aubrey. *Assessing Prior Learning—A CAEL Student Guide.* Columbia, Maryland: Cooperative Assessment of Experiential Learning, 1977.

Foster, Gerald P., et al. "Improving the Management of Nonprofit Enterprises: A Curriculum Approach." In *New Partnerships: Higher Education and the Nonprofit Sector. New Directions for Experiential Learning,* Vol. 18. San Francisco: Jossey-Bass Inc., 1982.

Fox, David B. "Academic Credit for Experiential Learning in Psychology: Learning Through Doing." Paper presented at the 89th Annual Convention of the American Psychological Association, Los Angeles, August 24-26, 1981.

Fremer, John. *Setting and Evaluating Criterion Standards in Implementing a Program for Assessment of Prior Learning. A CAEL Project Report.* Columbia, Maryland: Cooperative Assessment of Experiential Learning, 1976.

Fry, Ronald, and David Kolb. "Experiential Learning Theory and Learning/Experiences in Liberal Arts Education." In *Enriching the Liberal Arts through Experiential Learning. New Directions for Experiential Learning,* Vol. 6. San Francisco: Jossey-Bass Inc., 1979.

Fugate, Mary, and Terence MacTaggart. "Managing the Assessment Function." In *Cost-Effective Assessment of Prior Learning. New Directions for Experiential Learning,* Vol. 19. San Francisco: Jossey-Bass Inc., 1983.

Gagnon-Tremblay, Monique. "Dimensions of Equality: A Federal Government Work Plan for Women." Paper presented at the annual First Ministers' conference, Vancouver, November 20-21, 1986.

Goerke, Glenn A. "Certification of Noncredit Instruction." In *Developing New Adult Clienteles by Recognizing Prior Learning. New Directions for Experiential Learning,* Vol. 7. San Francisco: Jossey-Bass Inc., 1980.

Gold, Gerard G. "Editor's Notes." In *Business and Higher Education: Toward New Alliances. New Directions for Experiential Learning,* Vol. 13. San Francisco: Jossey-Bass Inc., 1981a.

—————. "Toward Business—Higher Education Alliances." In *Business and Higher Education: Toward New Alliances. New Directions for Experiential Learning,* Vol. 13. San Francisco: Jossey-Bass Inc., 1981b.

—————. "Closing Thoughts." In *Business and Higher Education: Toward New Alliances. New Directions for Experiential Learning,* Vol. 13. San Francisco: Jossey-Bass Inc., 1981c.

Goldsmith, Joan. "Competence Assessment within a Professional Training Program." In *Defining and Measuring Competence. New Directions for Experiential Learning,* Vol. 3. San Francisco: Jossey-Bass Inc., 1979.

Goldsmith, Joan, and Paul S. Pottinger. "Future Directions." In *Defining and Measuring Competence. New Directions for Experiential Learning,* Vol. 3. San Francisco: Jossey-Bass Inc., 1979.

Goldstein, Michael B. "Achieving the Nondiscriminatory Recognition of Experiential Learning." In *Learning by Experience—What, Why, How. New Directions for Experiential Learning,* Vol. 1. San Francisco: Jossey-Bass Inc., 1978.

Gould, Samuel B. "Future Directions for Prior Learning Programs." In *Developing New Adult Clienteles by Recognizing Prior Learning.*

New Directions for Experiential Learning, Vol. 7. San Francisco: Jossey-Bass Inc., 1980.

Gray, Lois, and Walter Davis. "Labor and Higher Education: Impetus to New Alliances." In *Building New Alliances: Labor Unions and Higher Education. New Directions for Experiential Learning,* Vol. 10. San Francisco: Jossey-Bass Inc., 1980.

Green, M.H., and J.J. Sullivan. "Credit for Noncollegiate Learning." *Educational Record,* Fall 1975: 257-261.

Greenberg, Elinor Miller. "Editor's Notes." In *New Partnerships: Higher Education and the Nonprofit Sector. New Directions for Experiential Learning,* Vol. 18. San Francisco: Jossey-Bass Inc., 1982.

Greenblatt, Arthur, and James Striby. "Outcomes for the Learning Artist." In *Clarifying Learning Outcomes in the Liberal Arts. New Directions for Experiential Learning,* Vol. 12. San Francisco: Jossey-Bass Inc., 1981.

Gross, Ron, et al. *Independent, Self-Directed Learners in American Life: The Other 80 Percent Learning.* Washington: George Washington University, Institute for Educational Leadership, 1977.

Haines, Pamela, and Robert Schwoebel. "Developing Self-Directed Learners in the Service Economy." In *Building on Experiences in Adult Development. New Directions for Experiential Learning,* Vol. 16. San Francisco: Jossey-Bass Inc., 1982.

Harris, J., and W. Troutt. "Educational Credentials: Past, Present, and Future." In *Educational Accomplishments.* Edited by J.W. Miller and 0. Mills. Washington: American Council on Education, 1978.

Hatala, Robert J. "Award and Transfer of Experiential Credits in Undergraduate Fields." In *Transferring Experiential Credit. New Directions for Experiential Learning,* Vol. 4. San Francisco: Jossey-Bass Inc., 1979.

—————. "A Problem-Solving Model of Graduate Education." In *Expanding the Missions of Graduate and Professional Education. New Directions for Experiential Learning,* Vol. 15. San Francisco: Jossey-Bass Inc., 1982.

Haugsby, Thomas R. "Preparing for Panoramic Careers." In *Combining Career Development with Experiential Learning. New Directions for Experiential Learning,* Vol. 5. San Francisco: Jossey-Bass Inc., 1979.

Heeger, Gerald A. "Marketing Prior Learning Assessment Programs." In *Cost-Effective Assessment of Prior Learning. New Directions for Experiential Learning,* Vol. 19. San Francisco: Jossey-Bass Inc., 1983.

Heermann, Barry. "Experiential Learning in the Community College." Topical Paper No. 63. California University. Los Angeles: ERIC Clearinghouse for Junior College Information, 1977.

Heermann, Barry, et al. "Program Initiation and Implementation: Three Diaries of Practice." In *Financing and Implementing Prior Learning Assessment. New Directions for Experiential Learning*, Vol. 14. San Francisco: Jossey-Bass Inc., 1981.

Henderson, Harold L., and Steven Hyre. "Contract Learning." In *Enriching the Liberal Arts through Experiential Learning. New Directions for Experiential Learning*, Vol. 6. San Francisco: Jossey-Bass Inc., 1979.

Hengesbach, Ted. *College Credit for Prior Learning: A Student Handbook.* South Bend, Indiana: Indiana University, 1979.

Hodgkinson, Harold L. "Preface." In *Business and Higher Education: Toward New Alliances. New Directions for Experiential Learning*, Vol. 13. San Francisco: Jossey-Bass Inc., 1981.

Hogan, Daniel B. "Is Licensing Public Protection or Professional Protectionalism?" In *Defining and Measuring Competence. New Directions for Experiential Learning*, Vol. 3. San Francisco: Jossey-Bass Inc., 1979.

Holt, Margaret. "Designing Programs for Returning Women Students." In *Building on Experiences in Adult Development. New Directions for Experiential Learning*, Vol. 16. San Francisco: Jossey-Bass Inc., 1982.

Hrudy, Norbert J. "The Faculty as Key to Quality Assurance—Fact and Mystique." In *Defining and Assuring Quality in Experiential Learning. New Directions for Experiential Learning*, Vol. 9. San Francisco: Jossey-Bass Inc., 1980.

Jacobs, Frederic. "Experiential Programs in Practice: Lessons to Be Learned." In *Expanding the Missions of Graduate and Professional Education. New Directions for Experiential Learning*, Vol. 15. San Francisco: Jossey-Bass Inc., 1982.

Jacobs, Frederic, and Richard J. Allen. "Editor's Notes." In *Expanding the Missions of Graduate and Professional Education. New Directions for Experiential Learning*, Vol. 15. San Francisco: Jossey-Bass Inc., 1982.

Jamison, Dean T., and Barbara Burgess Wolfe. "Assessment and Accreditation: Economic Considerations." In *Implementing a Program for Assessing Experiential Learning, A CAEL Project Report.* Princeton: Cooperative Assessment of Experiential Learning, 1976.

Johnson, Elmina C., and Louis G. Tornatzky. "Academia and Industrial Innovation." In *Business and Higher Education: Toward New Alliances. New Directions for Experiential Learning*, Vol. 13. San Francisco: Jossey-Bass Inc., 1981.

Keeton, Morris T. "Assuring the Quality of Educational Programs." In *Learning by Experience—What, Why, How. New Directions for Experiential Learning,* Vol. 1. San Francisco: Jossey-Bass Inc., 1978.

————. "Defining and Assuring Quality: A Framework of Questions." In *Defining and Assuring Quality in Experiential Learning. New Directions for Experiential Learning,* Vol. 9. San Francisco: Jossey-Bass Inc., 1980.

————. "On 'Scholarship for Society': A Decade Later." In *Expanding the Missions of Graduate and Professional Education. New Directions for Experiential Learning,* Vol. 15. San Francisco: Jossey-Bass Inc., 1982.

————. "Experiential Learning—Council for the Advancement of Experiential Learning and Quebec Colleges." *Études et Réflexions.* Fédération des Cégeps, Secteur Développement et Communications, 1, 1 (April 25, 1985).

Keeton, Morris T., and Pamela J. Tate. "Editor's Notes: The Boom in Experiential Learning." In *Learning by Experience—What, Why, How. New Directions for Experiential Learning,* Vol. 1. San Francisco: Jossey-Bass Inc., 1978a.

————. "What Next in Experiential Learning?" In *Learning by Experience—What, Why, How. New Directions for Experiential Learning,* Vol. 1. San Francisco: Jossey-Bass Inc., 1978b.

Kelly, Dorothy Ann. "College of New Rochelle's Response to: 'Adult Learning, Higher Education, and the Economics of Unused Capacity,' by Howard R. Bowen." Paper presented at the 1980 National Forum and Annual Business Meeting of the College Board and the College Scholarship Service, New York, October 27, 1980.

Kintzer, Frederick C. "Problems in Awarding and Transferring Experiential Learning Credits." In *Transferring Experiential Credit. New Directions for Experiential Learning,* Vol. 4. San Francisco: Jossey-Bass Inc., 1979.

Klemp, George O., Jr. "Identifying, Measuring and Integrating Competence." In *Defining and Measuring Competence. New Directions for Experiential Learning,* Vol. 3. San Francisco: Jossey-Bass Inc., 1979.

————. "Assessing Student Potential: An Immodest Proposal." In *Diverse Student Preparation: Benefits and Issues. New Directions for Experiential Learning,* Vol. 17. San Francisco: Jossey-Bass Inc., 1982.

Knapp, Joan. *Assessing Prior Learning—A CAEL Handbook.* Columbia, Maryland: Cooperative Assessment of Experiential Learning, 1977.

————. "Do Graduate Schools Discount Experiential Learning Credits?" In *Transferring Experiential Credit. New Directions for Experiential Learning,* Vol. 4. San Francisco: Jossey-Bass Inc., 1979.

Knapp, Joan. "Editor's Notes." In *Financing and Implementing Prior Learning Assessment. New Directions for Experiential Learning*, Vol. 14. San Francisco: Jossey-Bass Inc., 1981.

——————. "Assessing Experiential Learning in Graduate and Professional Education." In *Expanding the Missions of Graduate and Professional Education. New Directions for Experiential Learning*, Vol. 15. San Francisco: Jossey-Bass Inc., 1982.

Knapp, Joan, and Leta Davis. "Scope and Varieties of Experiential Learning." In *Learning by Experience—What, Why, How. New Directions for Experiential Learning*, Vol. 1. San Francisco: Jossey-Bass Inc., 1978.

Knapp, Joan, and Marianne Gardiner. "Assessment of Prior Learning: As a Model and in Practice." In *Financing and Implementing Prior Learning Assessment. New Directions for Experiential Learning*, Vol. 14. San Francisco: Jossey-Bass Inc., 1981.

Knapp, Joan, and Paul I. Jacobs. *Setting Standards for Assessing Experiential Learning*. Council for the Advancement of Experiential Learning, Columbia, Maryland. Princeton: ERIC Clearinghouse on Tests, Measurement, and Evaluation, 1981.

Knapp, Joan, and Amiel Sharon. *A Compendium of Assessment Techniques*. Columbia, Maryland: Cooperative Assessment of Experiential Learning, 1975.

Kolb, David A., and Linda H. Lewis. *Facilitating Experiential Learning— Observations and Reflections. New Directions for Continuing Education*. San Francisco: Jossey-Bass Inc., 1986.

Kray, Eugene J. *Faculty Attitudes toward Assessment of Experiential Learning*. Fort Lauderdale: Nova University, 1975.

Krueger, Brenda. "Improving the Credit for Lifelong Learning Process with Holistic Education Techniques." In *Building on Experiences in Adult Development. New Directions for Experiential Learning*, Vol. 16. San Francisco: Jossey-Bass Inc., 1982.

Kruh, Robert F. "Outlook for Graduate Education." In *Expanding the Missions of Graduate and Professional Education. New Directions for Experiential Learning*, Vol. 15. San Francisco: Jossey-Bass Inc., 1982.

Kurtz, Edwin B., Jr. "A Key to Quality Assurance: Clarifying Learning Outcomes." In *Defining and Assuring Quality in Experiential Learning. New Directions for Experiential Learning*, Vol. 9. San Francisco: Jossey-Bass Inc., 1980.

Kyle, Regina M.J. "Partners in Economic Development." In *Business and Higher Education: Toward New Alliances. New Directions for Experiential Learning*, Vol. 13. San Francisco: Jossey-Bass Inc., 1981.

Lamdin, Lois. "Teaching Strategies." In *Diverse Student Preparation: Benefits and Issues. New Directions for Experiential Learning,* Vol. 17. San Francisco: Jossey-Bass Inc., 1982.

Lapine, Louise, and Sandra Smith Moore. *Off-Campus Experimental Learning for Women: A Model Program.* Milwaukee: Alverno Research Center on Women, 1976.

Laudeman, Kent A. "Preparing for Experience through Self-Assessment." In *Combining Career Development with Experiential Learning. New Directions for Experiential Learning,* Vol. 5. San Francisco: Jossey-Bass Inc., 1979.

Lehman, T. "Evaluation Contract Learning." In *Current Issues in Higher Education: Learner-Centered Reform.* Edited by D.W. Vermilye. San Francisco: Jossey-Bass Inc., 1975.

Levine, Herbert, and Carroll M. Hutton. "Financing Labor's Role in Education and Training." In *Building New Alliances: Labor Unions and Higher Education. New Directions for Experiential Learning,* Vol. 10. San Francisco: Jossey-Bass Inc., 1980.

Little, Thomas C. "The Institutional Context for Experiential Learning." In *Making Sponsored Experiential Learning Standard Practice. New Directions for Experiential Learning,* Vol. 20. San Francisco: Jossey-Bass Inc., 1983.

Loacker, Georgine. "Revitalizing the Academic Disciplines by Clarifying Outcomes." In *Clarifying Learning Outcomes in the Liberal Arts. New Directions for Experiential Learning,* Vol. 12. San Francisco: Jossey-Bass Inc., 1981.

Loacker, Georgine, and Ernest G. Palola. "Editor's Notes." In *Clarifying Learning Outcomes in the Liberal Arts. New Directions for Experiential Learning,* Vol. 12. San Francisco: Jossey-Bass Inc., 1981.

Luskin, Bernard J., and James Small. "Coastline Community College: An Idea Beyond Tradition." Paper presented at the Conference of the American Association for Higher Education, Washington, D.C., March 4-5, 1980.

Lynton, Ernest A. "Colleges, Universities, and Corporate Training." In *Business and Higher Education: Toward New Alliances. New Directions for Experiential Learning,* Vol. 13. San Francisco: Jossey-Bass Inc., 1981.

MacTaggart, Terence. "Editor's Notes." In *Cost-Effective Assessment of Prior Learning. New Directions for Experiential Learning,* Vol. 19. San Francisco: Jossey-Bass Inc., 1983a.

————. "A Primer on the Financial Management of Experiential Learning Assessment Programs." In *Cost-Effective Assessment of Prior*

Learning. New Directions for Experiential Learning, Vol. 19. San Francisco: Jossey-Bass Inc., 1983b.

MacTaggart, Terence. "Closing Thoughts and Further Resources." In *Cost-Effective Assessment of Prior Learning. New Directions for Experiential Learning,* Vol. 19. San Francisco: Jossey-Bass Inc., 1983c.

MacTaggart, Terence, and Joan Knapp. "Costing and Financing Prior Learning Programs." In *Financing and Implementing Prior Learning Assessment. New Directions for Experiential Learning,* Vol. 14. San Francisco: Jossey-Bass Inc., 1981.

Maehl, William H., Jr. "The Graduate Tradition and Experiential Learning." In *Expanding the Missions of Graduate and Professional Education. New Directions for Experiential Learning,* Vol. 15. San Francisco: Jossey-Bass Inc., 1982.

Mahoney, Frances A. "Guidance and Planning with Diversely Prepared Students." In *Diverse Student Preparation: Benefits and Issues. New Directions for Experiential Learning,* Vol. 17. San Francisco: Jossey-Bass Inc., 1982.

Marienau, Catherine, and Arthur W. Chickering. "Adult Development and Learning." In *Building on Experiences in Adult Development. New Directions for Experiential Learning,* Vol. 16. San Francisco: Jossey-Bass Inc., 1982.

Mark, M., and P. Dewess. "Recruitment, Retention and Alumni Development of Adult Learners through Assessment of Prior Learning." *Lifelong Learning,* 8, 1 (September 1984): 18-20.

Mark, Michael, and Betty Menson. "Using David Kolb's Experiential Learning Theory in Portfolio Development Courses." In *Building on Experiences in Adult Development. New Directions for Experiential Learning,* Vol. 16. San Francisco: Jossey-Bass Inc., 1982.

Markovich, Greg, and Joan S. Malling. "The Role of Information Systems in Managing Experiential Learning Assessment Programs." In *Cost-Effective Assessment of Prior Learning. New Directions for Experiential Learning,* Vol. 19. San Francisco: Jossey-Bass Inc., 1983.

Martorana, S.V., and Eileen Kuhns. "Editor's Notes." In *Transferring Experiential Credit. New Directions for Experiential Learning,* Vol. 4. San Francisco: Jossey-Bass Inc., 1979a.

————. "The Politics of Control of Credit for Experiential Learning." In *Transferring Experiential Credit. New Directions for Experiential Learning,* Vol. 4. San Francisco: Jossey-Bass Inc., 1979b.

Matusak, Larraine R. "What Next?" In *Financing and Implementing Prior Learning Assessment. New Directions for Experiential Learning,* Vol. 14. San Francisco: Jossey-Bass Inc., 1981.

Mauksch, Hans O. "Social Change and Learning Outcomes: A Planned Approach." In *Clarifying Learning Outcomes in the Liberal Arts. New Directions for Experiential Learning,* Vol. 12. San Francisco: Jossey-Bass Inc., 1981.

McClure, Larry. "Expanding the High School through Experience-Based Care Education." In *Combining Career Development with Experiential Learning. New Directions for Experiential Learning,* Vol. 5. San Francisco: Jossey-Bass Inc., 1979.

McCoy, P.C. "Johnston College: An Experimental Model." In *The New Colleges: Toward an Appraisal.* Edited by P.L. Dressel. Monograph 7. Iowa City: American College Testing Program, 1971.

McGarraghy, John J., and Kevin P. Reilly. "College Credit for Corporate Training." In *Business and Higher Education: Toward New Alliances. New Directions for Experiential Learning,* Vol. 13. San Francisco: Jossey-Bass Inc., 1981.

McIntyre, Valerie. "Faculty Development for Prior Learning Programs: The Essential Ingredients." In *Financing and Implementing Prior Learning Assessment. New Directions for Experiential Learning,* Vol. 14. San Francisco: Jossey-Bass Inc., 1981.

Menson, Betty. "Editor's Notes." In *Building on Experiences in Adult Development. New Directions for Experiential Learning,* Vol. 16. San Francisco: Jossey-Bass Inc., 1982a.

——. "Conclusions and Additional Resources." In *Building on Experiences in Adult Development. New Directions for Experiential Learning,* Vol. 16. San Francisco: Jossey-Bass Inc., 1982b.

Meyer, Peter. *Awarding College Credit for Non-College Learning.* San Francisco: Jossey-Bass Inc., 1976.

Moon, Rexford G., Jr., and Gene R. Hawes. "Editor's Notes." In *Developing New Adult Clienteles by Recognizing Prior Learning. New Directions for Experiential Learning,* Vol. 7. San Francisco: Jossey-Bass Inc., 1980.

Moreault, Pierre. "Panel sur les priorités d'action et de concertation." Colloque "Reconnaître les acquis expérientiels à l'Université . . . Pourquoi ? Comment ?" Université de Sherbrooke, Sherbrooke, 29-31 mai 1985. ("Panel discussion on the priorities for dialogue and action." Seminar at the colloquium: "Recognizing experiential learning in universities . . . Why? How?" The University of Sherbrooke, Sherbrooke, May 29-31, 1985.)

Munce, John W. "Taking Charge of Experience through Life/Work Planning." In *Combining Career Development with Experiential Learning. New Directions for Experiential Learning,* Vol. 5. San Francisco: Jossey-Bass Inc., 1979.

Neely, Margery A., and Diane Dees. "Unpaid to Salaried Employment: Strategies for Change." Workshop presented at the Annual Convention of the National Vocational Guidance Association, St. Louis, Missouri, April 12, 1981.

Neely, Margery A., and John D. Steffen. "Evaluating Women's Administrative Skills Gained through Volunteer Work: A Pilot Run." *Journal of Vocational Education Research,* 4, 4 (Fall 1979): 75-86.

Neff, Charles B. "Some Concluding Observations and Further Resources." In *Cross-Cultural Learning. New Directions for Experiential Learning,* Vol. 11. San Francisco: Jossey-Bass Inc., 1981.

Nickse, Ruth S. *Guidelines for Developing Alternative Adult Credentialing Programs.* Boston: Massachussetts State Department of Education, Bureau of Community Education and Adult Services, 1981.

O'Connell, Brian. "The Independent Sector: Uniquely American." In *New Partnerships: Higher Education and the Nonprofit Sector. New Directions for Experiential Learning,* Vol. 18. San Francisco: Jossey-Bass Inc., 1982.

O'Connell, William R., Jr. "Potential for Faculty Leadership in Transfer." In *Transferring Experiential Credit. New Directions for Experiential Learning,* Vol. 4. San Francisco: Jossey-Bass Inc., 1979.

Olson, Paul A., and Lawrence Freeman. "Defining Competence in Teacher Licensing Usage." In *Defining and Measuring Competence. New Directions for Experiential Learning,* Vol. 3. San Francisco: Jossey-Bass Inc., 1979.

Oxnard, Charles E. "Graduate Education and the New Experiential Learning." In *Expanding the Missions of Graduate and Professional Education. New Directions for Experiential Learning,* Vol. 15. San Francisco: Jossey-Bass Inc., 1982.

Pendergrass, Judith, et al. "The Interim and Related Procedure." In *Expert Assessment of Experiential Learning. A CAEL Handbook.* Columbia, Maryland: Cooperative Assessment of Experiential Learning, 1977.

Pottinger, Paul S., and Joan Goldsmith. "Editor's Notes." In *Defining and Measuring Competence. New Directions for Experiential Learning,* Vol. 3. San Francisco: Jossey-Bass Inc., 1979.

Presno, Vincent. "A Value Analysis of Historically Significant Forms of Subject Matter." Paper presented at the Annual Meeting of the American Educational Research Association, New York, March 19, 1982.

Preston, Kathleen. "Assessment of Prior Learning: An Interdisciplinary Perspective." Paper presented at the 89th Annual Meeting of the American Psychological Association, Los Angeles, August 1981.

Proffitt, John R., and Don Di Spirito. "Potential for Federal Leadership in a New Educational Direction: Experiential Learning." In *Transferring*

Experiential Credit. New Directions for Experiential Learning, Vol. 4. San Francisco: Jossey-Bass Inc., 1979.

Proulx, Jean. "La reconnaissance scolaire des acquis expérientiels: une double assise." Exposé. Colloque "Reconnaître les acquis expérientiels à l'Université . . . Pourquoi ? Comment ?" Université de Sherbrooke, Sherbrooke, 29-31 mai 1985. ("The recognition of experiential learning by educational institutions." Presentation given at the colloquium: "Recognizing experiential learning in universities . . . Why? How?" The University of Sherbrooke, Sherbrooke, May 29-31, 1985.)

Quebec. Ministère de l'Éducation. Bureau du sous-ministre, Comité de la coordination ministérielle de la reconnaissance des acquis de formation. *Plan d'action relatif à la reconnaissance des acquis de formation (1983-1986).* Québec, 14 février 1984. (Ministry of Education. Office of the Deputy Minister, Committee for the coordination of the recognition of prior learning. "Action plan with respect to the recognition of prior learning (1983-1986)." Quebec, February 14, 1984.)

—————. Ministère de l'Éducation. Comité de Coordination ministérielle. *Reconnaissance des acquis de formation. Communiqué 1.* Québec, janvier 1986. (Ministry of Education. Ministerial Coordination Committee. *The recognition of prior learning. Memorandum 1.* Quebec, January 1986.)

—————. Ministère de l'Éducation. Comité de Coordination ministérielle. *Reconnaissance des acquis de formation. Comuniqué 2.* Québec, mai 1986. (Ministry of Education. Ministerial Coordination Committee, *The recognition of prior learning. Memorandum 2.* Quebec, May 1986.)

Ranta, Richard R. "Crediting Prior Experiential Learning." Paper presented at the 66th Annual Meeting of the Speech Communication Association, New York, November 13-16, 1980.

Rawe, Lucy Ruth. "How Transcripts for Experiential Learning Assist in Articulation." In *Transferring Experiential Credit. New Directions for Experiential Learning,* Vol. 4. San Francisco: Jossey-Bass Inc., 1979.

Rawlings, Lyngrid S., and Jean B. Davison. *Program Design for External High School Diploma Program.* Washington, D.C.: District of Columbia Public Schools, 1980.

Ray, Garrett W. "Meeting Volunteers on Their Own Grounds." In *New Partnerships: Higher Education and the Nonprofit Sector. New Directions for Experiential Learning,* Vol. 18. San Francisco: Jossey-Bass Inc., 1982.

Reichlin, Seth. "Volunteering and Adult Education: A Historical View." In *New Partnerships: Higher Education and the Nonprofit Sector. New Directions for Experiential Learning,* Vol. 18. San Francisco: Jossey-Bass Inc., 1982.

Reilly, R., et al. *Expert Assessment of Experiential Learning—A CAEL Handbook. (Number 1)* Columbia, Maryland: Cooperative Assessment of Experiential Learning, 1977.

Reinharz, Shulamit. "Undergraduates as Experiential Learning Facilitators." In *Enriching the Liberal Arts through Experiential Learning. New Directions for Experiential Learning,* Vol. 6. San Francisco: Jossey-Bass Inc., 1979.

Riedel, J.E. *Student Handbook: Interdisciplinary Studies 800—Assessment of Experiential Learning.* Fountain Valley, California: Coastline Community College, 1978.

Rosenman, Mark. "Colleges and Social Change: Partnerships with Community-Based Organizations." In *New Partnerships: Higher Education and the Nonprofit Sector. New Directions for Experiential Learning,* Vol. 18. San Francisco: Jossey-Bass Inc., 1982.

Rosenstein, Paul, and Hal Stack. "Models of Union-University Cooperation." In *Building New Alliances: Labor Unions and Higher Education. New Directions for Experiential Learning,* Vol. 10. San Francisco: Jossey-Bass Inc., 1980.

Rubin, Sharon G. "The Dialogue Between Voluntarism and Feminism: Implications for Higher Education." In *New Partnerships: Higher Education and the Nonprofit Sector. New Directions for Experiential Learning,* Vol. 18. San Francisco: Jossey-Bass Inc., 1982.

Rydell, Susan T. *Creditable Portfolios: Dimensions in Diversity. A CAEL Resource Manual.* Columbia, Maryland: Council for Adult and Experiential Learning: 1982.

Sachs, Martha Pomeranz. "The Tasks of Administrators in Assuring Sound Assessment Practices." In *Defining and Assuring Quality in Experiential Learning. New Directions for Experiential Learning,* Vol. 9. San Francisco: Jossey-Bass Inc., 1980.

Sackmary, Benjamin, and Hannah Hedrick. "Assessment of the Experiential Learning of Women for College Credit in the Area of Women's Studies. (Preliminary Working Draft)." Paper presented at the National Conference of the Council for Adult and Experiential Learning, San Francisco, October 1977.

Sansregret, Marthe. "The Canadian Experience of Experiential Learning in Higher Education." Paper (co-sponsored by The British Council and SIACE) presented at the Access by Mature Students to Higher Education Conference held by the Scottish Institute of Adult and Continuing Education and the Association for Recurrent Education, Edinburgh, Scotland, October 29, 1986. Edinburgh: SIACE, 1986.

Schatz, Jack, et al. "Learners Assess the Prior Learning Assessment Process." In *Financing and Implementing Prior Learning Assessment.*

New Directions for Experiential Learning, Vol. 14. San Francisco: Jossey-Bass Inc., 1981.

Scott, Nancy A. *Returning Women Students: A Review of Research and Descriptive Studies.* Washington, D.C.: National Association for Women Deans, Administrators and Counselors, 1980.

Seeman, H. "A Rationale and Methodology for Assessing and Awarding Credit for Experiential Learning or for Cooperative Education Work Experience." *CVA/ACFP Journal,* 19, 3 (November 1983).

Serling, Albert M. "Credit for Learning: The Composite-Portfolio Model." In *Developing New Adult Clienteles by Recognizing Prior Learning. New Directions for Experiential Learning,* Vol. 7. San Francisco: Jossey-Bass Inc., 1980.

Sharon, Amiel T. *Assessing Occupational Competences—A CAEL Handbook.* Columbia, Maryland: Cooperative Assessment of Experiential Learning, 1977.

Sheckley, Barry, and Janet Warnet. "Budgeting for Experiential Learning Assessment Programs." In *Cost-Effective Assessment of Prior Learning. New Directions for Experiential Learning,* Vol. 19. San Francisco: Jossey-Bass Inc., 1983.

Shipton, Jane, and Elizabeth Steltenpohl. "Self-Directedness of the Learner as a Key to Quality Assurance." In *Defining and Assuring Quality in Experiential Learning. New Directions for Experiential Learning,* Vol. 9. San Francisco: Jossey-Bass Inc., 1980.

—————. "Relating Assessment of Prior Learning to Educational Planning." In *Financing and Implementing Prior Learning Assessment. New Directions for Experiential Learning,* Vol. 14. San Francisco: Jossey-Bass Inc., 1981.

Shulman, Carol Herrnstadt. "Implementing Experiential Learning for Adult Students." In *ERIC/Higher Education Research Currents.* Washington, D.C.: George Washington University, ERIC Clearinghouse on Higher Education, May 1978.

Silverman, Paul, and Pamela J. Tate. "The Accrediting Process as an Aid to Quality Assurance." In *Defining and Assuring Quality in Experiential Learning. New Directions for Experiential Learning,* Vol. 9. San Francisco: Jossey-Bass Inc., 1980.

Simosko, Susan. *Earn College Credit For What You Know.* Washington: Acropolis Books, 1985.

Singer, David L. "Professional Socialization and Adult Development in Graduate Professional Education." In *Building on Experiences in Adult Development. New Directions for Experiential Learning,* Vol. 16. San Francisco: Jossey-Bass Inc., 1982.

Smith, Howard A. "Toward a New Paradigm for Translating Theory into Practice." Proceedings of the Annual Midwest Research-to-Practice Conference in Adult Continuing Education, Ann Arbor School, Berlin, Michigan, October 10-11, 1985.

Smith, Lana I., and Dennie L. Smith. "Experiential Learning: Teaching Teachers to Transfer Their Knowledge." *Journal of Reading,* 8, 2 (January 1986): 20-24.

Smith, Peter. "Al, Elaine, Jennie, and Jack." In *Diverse Student Preparation: Benefits and Issues. New Directions for Experiential Learning,* Vol. 17. San Francisco: Jossey-Bass Inc., 1982.

Smythe, Ormond. "Practical Experience and the Liberal Arts: A Philosophical Perspective." In *Enriching the Liberal Arts through Experiential Learning. New Directions for Experiential Learning,* Vol. 6. San Francisco: Jossey-Bass Inc., 1979.

Smythe, Ormond, and Patricia L. Jerabek. "Faculty and Institutional Development: Bridging the Experience Gap." In *Diverse Student Preparation: Benefits and Issues. New Directions for Experiential Learning,* Vol. 17. San Francisco: Jossey-Bass Inc., 1982.

Spille, Henry. "Credit for Learning Gained in Military Service or Employment." In *Developing New Adult Clienteles by Recognizing Prior Learning. New Directions for Experiential Learning,* Vol. 7. San Francisco: Jossey-Bass Inc., 1980.

Spille, Henry, et al. "Assuring High Standards, Quality Control, and Consistency." In *Developing New Adult Clienteles by Recognizing Prior Learning. New Directions for Experiential Learning,* Vol. 7. San Francisco: Jossey-Bass Inc., 1980.

Stack, Hal, and Carroll M. Hutton. "Editor's Notes." In *Building New Alliances: Labor Unions and Higher Education. New Directions for Experiential Learning,* Vol. 10. San Francisco: Jossey-Bass Inc., 1980a.

————. "Conclusions and Further Resources." In *Building New Alliances: Labor Unions and Higher Education. New Directions for Experiential Learning,* Vol. 10. San Francisco: Jossey-Bass Inc., 1980b.

Stack, Hal, and Oscar Paskal. "The University Studies and Weekend College Program: Beyond Access." In *Building New Alliances: Labor Unions and Higher Education. New Directions for Experiential Learning,* Vol. 10. San Francisco: Jossey-Bass Inc., 1980.

Stanley, Elizabeth. "Credit for Prior or Experiential Learning." Information Series No. 210. Ohio State University, National Center for Research in Vocational Education. Columbus, Ohio: ERIC Clearinghouse on Adult, Career, and Vocational Education, 1980.

Stephens College Without Walls. *Prior Learning: A Guide to Portfolio Development.* Columbia, Missouri, 1977.

Stevens, Mary A. "Developing Learning Objectives for a Model Course to Prepare Adults for the Assessment of Prior, Non-Sponsored Learning by Portfolio Evaluation." Ed.D. dissertation, Nova University, Moline, Illinois, 1977.

Stoel, Carol F. "Improving Postsecondary Education Through the Nonprofit Sector." In *New Partnerships: Higher Education and the Nonprofit Sector. New Directions for Experiential Learning,* Vol. 18. San Francisco: Jossey-Bass Inc., 1982.

Strange, John. "Credit for Learning Gained in Life and Work Experience." In *Developing New Adult Clienteles by Recognizing Prior Learning. New Directions for Experiential Learning,* Vol. 7. San Francisco: Jossey-Bass Inc., 1980.

Sweet, David. "Building Adult Student Enrollment: Actions to Take Now." In *Developing New Adult Clienteles by Recognizing Prior Learning. New Directions for Experiential Learning,* Vol. 7. San Francisco: Jossey-Bass Inc., 1980.

Taaffee, Thomas, and Eleanor Litwak. "A Union Campus." In *Building New Alliances: Labor Unions and Higher Education. New Directions for Experiential Learning,* Vol. 10. San Francisco: Jossey-Bass Inc., 1980.

Taylor, Clark. "A New Agenda for the Experiential Learning Movement." In *Diverse Student Preparation: Benefits and Issues. New Directions for Experiential Learning,* Vol. 17. San Francisco: Jossey-Bass Inc., 1982a.

—————. "Editor's Notes: Preparation for College—Expanding the View and Keying on Strengths." In *Diverse Student Preparation: Benefit and Issues. New Directions for Experiential Learning,* Vol. 17. San Francisco: Jossey-Bass Inc., 1982b.

Thomas, Nina, et al. "Educational Information Centers: One Answer for Adults." In *Building on Experiences in Adult Development. New Directions for Experiential Learning,* Vol. 16. San Francisco: Jossey-Bass Inc., 1982.

Valley, John R. "Prior Learning Credit Programs: Financial Impact on the College." In *Developing New Adult Clienteles by Recognizing Prior Learning. New Directions for Experiential Learning,* Vol. 7. San Francisco: Jossey-Bass Inc., 1980.

Van Aalst, Frank D. "Career Development Theory and Practice." In *Combining Career Development with Experiential Learning. New Directions for Experiential Learning,* Vol. 5. San Francisco: Jossey-Bass Inc., 1979.

Ward, Barbara. "Credit for Learning: The Competence-Based Model." In *Developing New Adult Clienteles by Recognizing Prior Learning. New Directions for Experiential Learning,* Vol. 7. San Francisco: Jossey-Bass Inc., 1980.

Warren, Jonathan. "Awarding Credit for Non-Traditional Programs." In *Transferring Experiential Credit. New Directions for Experiential Learning,* Vol. 4. San Francisco: Jossey-Bass Inc., 1979.

Warren, R.J., and P.W. Breen. *The Educational Value of Portfolio and Learning Contract Development.* Columbia, Maryland: Council for the Advancement of Experiential Learning, 1981.

Watkins, Ed. "Developing Careers in College." In *Combining Career Development with Experiential Learning. New Directions for Experiential Learning,* Vol. 5. San Francisco: Jossey-Bass Inc., 1979.

Whitaker, Urban G. "Assessors and Their Qualifications." In *Experiential Learning, Rationale, Characteristics, and Assessment.* Edited by M.T. Keeton and Associates. San Francisco: Jossey-Bass Inc., 1976.

————. "Equipping Faculty for Their Emerging Role as Experiential Educators." In *Learning by Experience—What, Why, How. New Directions for Experiential Learning,* Vol. 1. San Francisco: Jossey-Bass Inc., 1978.

————. *Assessing Learning — Standards, Principles, & Procedures.* Philadelphia: Council for Adult and Experiential Learning, 1989.

Willingham, Warren W. *Principles of Good Practice in Assessing Experiential Learning.* Princeton: Cooperative Assessment of Experiential Learning Project, 1977.

Willingham, Warren W., and K.F. Geisinger. *Project Report: Implementing a Program for Assessment of Experiential Learning.* Columbia, Maryland: Cooperative Assessment of Experiential Learning, 1976.

Willingham, Warren W., and Hadley S. Nesbitt. *Implementing a Program for Assessing Experiential Learning. A CAEL Project Report.* Columbia, Maryland: Cooperative Assessment of Experiential Learning, 1976.

Wingard, Edward. "The Experience of the Historically Black Colleges in Serving Diversely Prepared Students." In *Diverse Student Preparation: Benefits and Issues. New Directions for Experiential Learning,* Vol. 17. San Francisco: Jossey-Bass Inc., 1982.

Withorn, Ann, and Loretta Cedrone. "Assessing Ourselves: The Experience of the College of Public and Community Services." In *Defining and Measuring Competence. New Directions for Experiential Learning,* Vol. 3. San Francisco: Jossey-Bass Inc., 1979.

Witkowski, Edward. "The Individual and Social Benefits of Experiential Learning Assessment." In *Cost-Effective Assessment of Prior Learning.*

New Directions for Experiential Learning, Vol. 19. San Francisco: Jossey-Bass Inc., 1983.

Wolfe, Donald M. "Developing Professional Competence in the Applied Behavioral Sciences." In *Developing Experiential Learning Programs for Professional Education. New Directions for Experiential Learning,* Vol. 8. San Francisco: Jossey-Bass Inc., 1980.

Wolfe, Douglas E., and Eugene T. Byrne. "An Experiential MBA Program: Results of an Experiment." In *Developing Experiential Learning Programs for Professional Education. New Directions for Experiential Learning,* Vol. 8. San Francisco: Jossey-Bass Inc., 1980.

Wolff, Ralph A. "Alternative Models of Self-Study—New Approaches to Systematic Quality Assurance." In *Defining and Assuring Quality in Experiential Learning. New Directions for Experiential Learning,* Vol. 9. San Francisco: Jossey-Bass Inc., 1980.

Young, Kenneth E., and Grover J. Andrews. "Potential for Leadership by Accrediting Agencies." In *Transferring Experiential Credit. New Directions for Experiential Learning,* Vol. 4. San Francisco: Jossey-Bass Inc., 1979.

Adult Education

Axford, Roger W. *Adult Education: The Open Door to Lifelong Learning.* Indiana: A.G. Halladin Publishing Co., 1980.

Bergevin, P. *A Philosophy for Adult Education.* New York: The Seabury Press, 1967.

Bloom, Benjamin D., et al. *Taxonomy of Educational Objectives: Handbook 1, Cognitive Domain.* New York: David McKay Co. Inc., 1956.

Boucouvalas, Marcie. "Social Transformation, Lifelong Learning and the Fourth Force—Transpersonal Psychology." *Lifelong Learning, The Adult Years,* American Association for Adult and Continuing Education, March 1983.

Coleman, J.S., et al. "The Hopkins Games Programme: Conclusions from Seven Years of Research." *Educational Research,* 2 (1973): 3-7.

Dewey, John. *Experience and Education.* London: Collier, MacMillan, 1938.

Elias, John L., and Sharon Merriam. *Penser l'éducation des adultes.* Transl. A. Chené and E. Ollivier. Montreal: Ed. Guerin Montréal-Toronto, 1980.

Erikson, E. *Identity, Youth and Crisis.* New York: Norton Inc., 1968.

Kanfer, F.W., and A.P. Goldstein. *Helping People Change. A Textbook of Methods. Pergamon General Psychology Series.* New York: Pergamon Press Inc., 1975.

Knowles, Malcolm S. *The Modern Practice of Adult Education: Andragogy vs. Pedagogy.* Chicago: Associated Press, Follett Publishing Company, 1970.

—————. *The Adult Learner: A Neglected Species.* Houston: Gulf Publishing Co., 1978.

Knox, A.B. *Adult Development and Change.* San Francisco: Jossey-Bass Publishers, 1977.

Kolb, David A. *Learning Styles Inventory: Self-Scoring Test and Interpretation Booklet.* Boston: McBer & Co., 1976.

Krathwohl, David R., et al. *Taxonomie des objectifs pédagogiques, Tome 2, Domaine affectif.* ("Taxonomy of educational objectives, volume 2, The affective domain.") Transl. Marcel Lavallée. Quebec: Les Presses de l'Université du Québec, 1980.

Lawson, K.H. *Philosophical Concepts and Values in Adult Education.* Department of Adult Education, University of Nottingham in association with the National Institute of Adult Education. Nottingham: Barnes and Humby Ltd., 1975.

Magarell, J. "The Enrollment Boom Among Older Americans: One in Three College Students is Now Over Twenty-Five Years Old." *Chronicle of Higher Education,* 22, 11 (May 4, 1981): 3.

Maslow, A.H. *Motivation and Personality.* Second Edition. New York: Harper & Row Publishers, 1970.

McClelland, D.C. *The Behavioral Event Interview Technique.* Boston: McBer & Co., 1976.

Overly, N.V., et al. "A Model for Lifelong Learning: Phi Delta Kappa." Commission on Lifelong Learning. *Phi Delta Kappan,* 1 (1980).

Penland, P.R. *Individual Self-Planned Learning in America.* Pittsburgh: Graduate School of Library and Information Sciences, University of Pittsburgh, 1977.

Quebec. Ministère de l'Éducation. Commission d'Études sur la Formation des Adultes (CÉFA). *La reconnaissance des acquis: un point de départ et d'arrivée du décloisonnement.* Québec, 1982. (Ministry of Education. Study commission on adult education. *The recognition of prior learning: the point of departure and the arrival of de-compartmentalization.* Quebec, 1982.)

—————. Ministère de l'Éducation. Direction des politiques et des plans. *Mémoire.* Québec, avril 1983. (Ministry of Education. Policy and planning management. *Report.* Quebec, April 1983.)

Schaeffer, R.G., and E.F. Lynton. *Corporate Experience in Improving Women's Job Opportunities.* New York: The Conference Board Inc., 1979.

Tétrault, Raymond. "Maslow, d'hier à aujourd'hui." ("Maslow, from yester-
day to today.") Université de Montréal, F.E.S., Section andragogie,
September 1985.

Tough, A. *Major Learning Efforts: Recent Research and Future Decisions.*
Toronto: Ontario Institute for Studies in Education, 1977.

United Nations Educational, Scientific and Cultural Organization. *Qua-
trième Conférence Internationale sur l'Éducation des Adultes.
(Fourth international conference on adult education.)* Paris, 1985.

Other References

Alpalhaô, Joaô Antonio. "La Psychosynthèse de Roberto Assagioli, Cadre
systématique, visée éducative, approche pastorale." ("The Psychosyn-
thesis of Roberto Assagioli, Systematic framework, educational aim,
pastoral approach.") Ph.D. dissertation, Université de Montréal, 1986.

Dictionnaire de philosophie. Edited by Gérard Legrand. Paris: Bordas,
1983.

Dictionnaire encyclopédique Larousse. Paris: Librairie Larousse, 1979.

Dictionnaire encyclopédique universel. Volume 8. Paris: Librairie Aristide
Quillet, 1962.

Lalande, André. *Vocabulaire technique et critique de la philosophie.* (Technical and critical vocabulary of philosophy.) Paris: Presses
Universitaires de France, 1972.

Lauffer, A., and A. Gorodezky. *Volunteers.* Beverly Hills: Sage, 1977.

Oxford English Dictionary. The Compact Edition. Volume II. U.S.A. Sup-
plement and Bibliography. London: Oxford University Press, 1971.

Rehnborg, S. "A Two-Way Street." *Voluntary Action Leadership,* 28 (Fall
1979): 28-30.

Robert, Paul. *Dictionnaire alphabétique et analogique de la langue
française. Les mots et les associations d'idées.* (Alphabetical and
analogical French dictionary. Words and the association of ideas.)
Tome 5. Paris: Le Robert, 1978.

Straus, E.S. *The Volunteer Professional.* New York: Straus Communications Inc., 1972.

Thornton, S. *1981 Littleton Leadership Proceedings.* Littleton, Colorado,
1981.

Toffler, Alvin. *The Future Shock.* New York: Random House Inc., 1970.

Webster's New Twentieth Century Dictionary. Second Edition. New York:
The Publisher's Guild, 1956.

About the Author

Before she reached the age of twenty, Marthe Sansregret had completed a university degree in Canada. She followed up this achievement with two more years of training in the United States. Back in Montreal, she worked at the United States Consulate General and then took a sabbatical year in Europe. Upon her return to Canada, the author began working in private business and did so for fifteen years.

A mother of two sons and a volunteer, the author later returned to school and earned her Bachelor of Science and Master of Arts degrees. She then obtained her doctoral degree (Ph.D.) from the University of Montreal after conducting extensive research in the United States. An international consultant in Prior Learning Assessment, the author lectures at several universities. She has received a number of mentions and honors, most notably from the American Biographical Institute in Raleigh, North Carolina, and from the International Biographical Center in Cambridge, England.

- Cap-Saint-Ignace
- Sainte-Marie (Beauce)
Québec, Canada
1995